TEACHNIQUES

Creative Designs for Teachers of Youth and Adults

JACK RENARD PRESSEAU

D1518789

John Knox Press
ATLANTA

ACKNOWLEDGMENTS

Many people helped to bring this book to fruition.

I was able to enjoy a writing sabbatical during the winter term, 1978, to begin this book because of the kindness of two of my colleagues at Presbyterian College. Dr. Lennart Pearson, Head Librarian, simply volunteered to teach my two sections of "Freshman Bible" (New Testament) and Miss Marion Hill, Associate Dean of Students, with whom I regularly co-teach "The Christian Education of Children and Families," virtually took over that course except for several lectures. Since Presbyterian College released me from the responsibility of a fourth section or course that term, my schedule was fully cleared and I made this book my primary responsibility. To adapt a biblical truism, "Greater love hath no one than this, that he/she teach a course for a colleague."

I was wisely and patiently counseled by Dr. Richard Ray and Mr. R. Donald Hardy, Jr., of John Knox Press, who assigned me an excellent copy editor, Eva Stimson. Efficient typing was done by Sandra Maceyko, my student secretary; Mrs. Pat Brunson; and, principally, Mmes. Ann Martin and Debbie Fravel. Critic readers, some of whom I do not even know (secured by the editors at John Knox) focused light on my blind spots in most helpful ways. Finally, my wife Jane, Student Services Librarian at Presbyterian College, found the things I needed, proofed and critiqued the manuscript, and shared with me the vision that this book had a ministry to perform.

Library of Congress Cataloging in Publication Data

Presseau, Jack Renard, 1933–
    Teachniques : creative designs for teachers of youth and adults.

    1. Christian education—Teaching methods.
I. Title.
BV1534.P73   1982   268'.6   81-85331
ISBN 0-8042-1414-X

DEDICATION

To LENNART and MARION

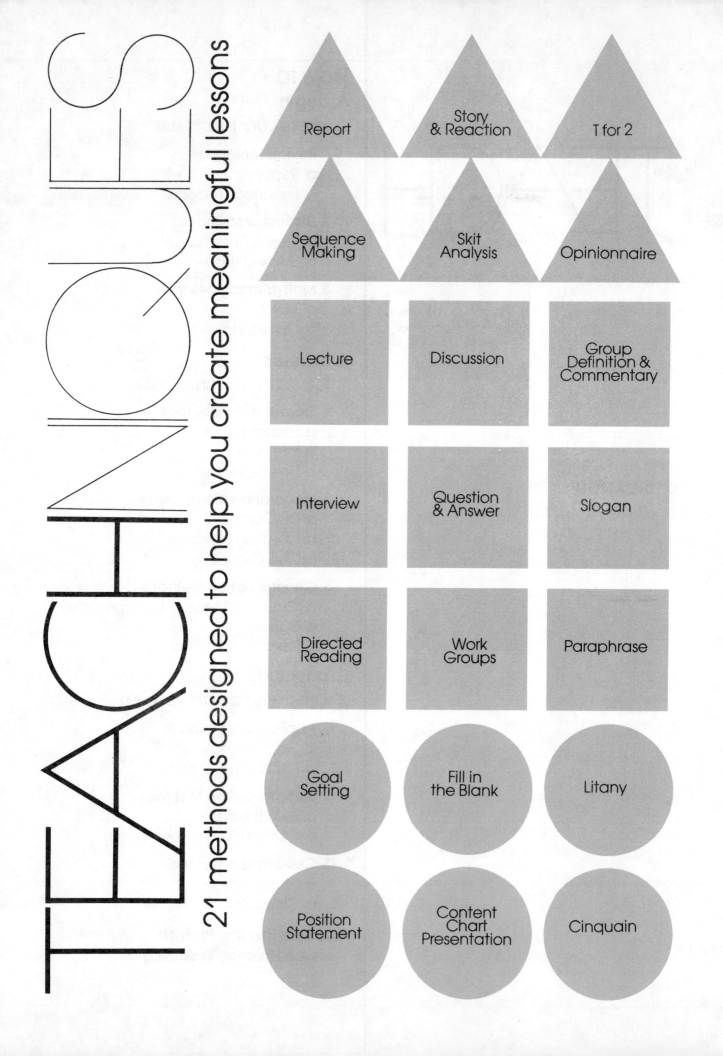

TEACHNIQUES

21 methods designed to help you create meaningful lessons

Report

Story & Reaction

T for 2

Sequence Making

Skit Analysis

Opinionnaire

Lecture

Discussion

Group Definition & Commentary

Interview

Question & Answer

Slogan

Directed Reading

Work Groups

Paraphrase

Goal Setting

Fill in the Blank

Litany

Position Statement

Content Chart Presentation

Cinquain

HOW TO
use these methods to teach creatively

Each Thursday I used to draw .25 cc. of serum from a vial kept cool in the refrigerator. I'd hand the syringe to my daughter who would dab some alcohol on my arm and deftly (most of the time) give me a shot. Observers said that it looked as easy as when the nurses did it. Then I'd load up another syringe and "shoot" her.

However, I shall never forget the time in our allergy program when it was decided that, having an emergency overdose kit on hand, we could give most of our own injections. We'd seen the nurses do it hundreds of times. But, when the realization that we would soon be shooting each other hit us, we paid serious attention to the nurse's technique and flat out asked her, "Okay, what's the system?"

You've probably been a participant and observer in many church school classes over a period of years. You've experienced some lessons which flew by and others which felt like an "in-terminal" illness. But, now you know that in a matter of months, weeks, or even days *you* will be "on." You're watching those who teach well and with apparent effortlessness in a new way—with anxiety—motivated interest! The question foremost in your mind is, **"What's the system?"**

The point of my analogy has nothing to do with learning how to painlessly inject knowledge into church school students without overdosing them. Nor does it have to do with immunizing students against worldliness or keeping them from sneezing at Christianity. My contention is that when you uttered those two life-changing words, "I'll teach," you became as concerned with surviving as you are with being able to communicate. A simple answer to, "What's the system?" is what will enable you to replace your anxiety with a good measure of healthy self-confidence.

To give you "the system" is the object of this book. Three techniques will be used to simplify this process.

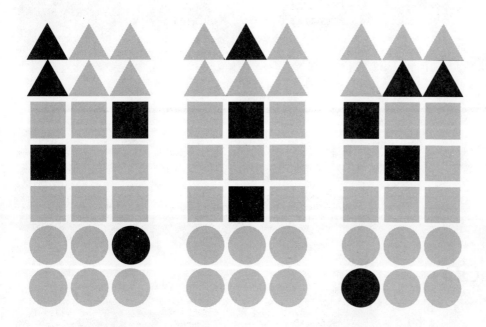

A

begin
where your
pupils are

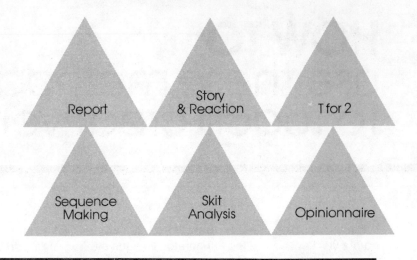

Report | Story & Reaction | T for 2

Sequence Making | Skit Analysis | Opinionnaire

B

develop
the lesson
meaningfully

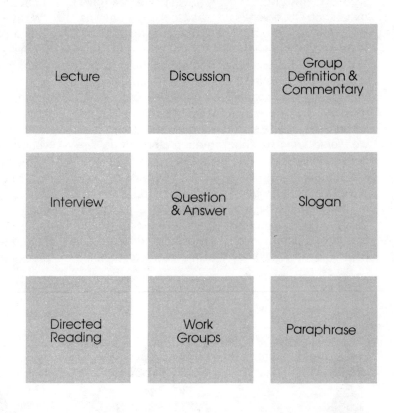

Lecture	Discussion	Group Definition & Commentary
Interview	Question & Answer	Slogan
Directed Reading	Work Groups	Paraphrase

C

conclude
with precision
and power

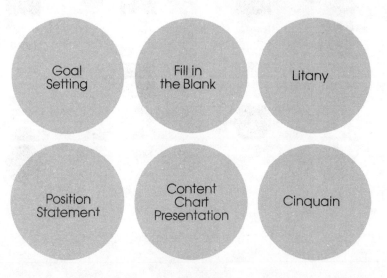

| Goal Setting | Fill in the Blank | Litany |
| Position Statement | Content Chart Presentation | Cinquain |

SIMPLIFICATION TECHNIQUE ONE:
Slow It Down!

A magician keeps the audience amazed because the critical moves are often made extremely quickly while people's attention has been diverted elsewhere. If you could watch the act repeatedly, giving attention to different segments of the action, you'd probably learn which moves were for show, or distraction, and which caused the trick to work.

Teaching is also demystified when you know what to look for and what to ignore (at least temporarily). I have sent students out to observe classes two ways: first they were told to "observe" and write up what they saw; for the second go-round they were given a specific list of things to look for to enable them to spot the structure in the sessions. They tell me, "When you know where the really important action is, it's much easier to see it. It's not as much fun as discovering it yourself, but it sure is more efficient!"

This second method of observation might not seem like slowing down the action the way you do when you run the film of a sports play in slow motion. However, giving your full attention to only that which is of critical importance has the same effect because your mind has less information to process in any one time period.

Thus, this book simplifies the teaching process by ignoring much and focusing on the heart of what the teacher actually does: choose and *use methods* (utilizing resources to achieve lesson objectives). That basic system of how methods are selected to communicate the content of our faith is the sole object of our attention.

SIMPLIFICATION TECHNIQUE TWO:
Break It Down!

You'll have a second plus going for you, besides being able to "slow it down." Unlike swimming and pole vaulting, classroom teaching is an activity which can be broken down and studied in parts. We'll do that in two ways.

The first breakdown of the lesson is into its three phases:

A. BEGIN the lesson

B. DEVELOP the lesson

C. CONCLUDE the lesson

A chapter will be devoted to each of these phases because each has a unique function.

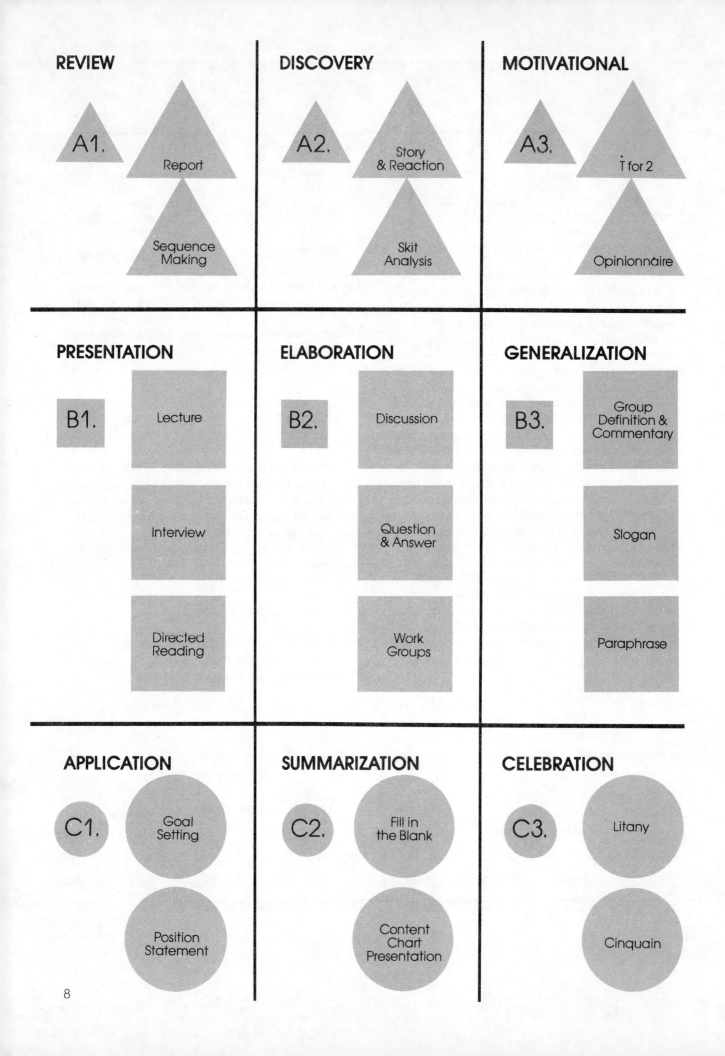

REVIEW

A1.

Report

Sequence Making

DISCOVERY

A2.

Story & Reaction

Skit Analysis

MOTIVATIONAL

A3.

T for 2

Opinionnaire

PRESENTATION

B1.

Lecture

Interview

Directed Reading

ELABORATION

B2.

Discussion

Question & Answer

Work Groups

GENERALIZATION

B3.

Group Definition & Commentary

Slogan

Paraphrase

APPLICATION

C1.

Goal Setting

Position Statement

SUMMARIZATION

C2.

Fill in the Blank

Content Chart Presentation

CELEBRATION

C3.

Litany

Cinquain

A second breakdown is the subdivision of each phase into three categories of teaching methods. Consult the chart on the opposite page. Note that at the top of each block is a category name. In the "BEGIN" phase the category divisions are based on the class's knowledge and motivation. The categories of the "DEVELOP" phase focus on things you must consider doing with the content of the lesson, such as presenting it, examining its meaning, and/or getting it into a principle. The "CONCLUDE" phase categories ask you to decide whether the most appropriate ending is an application to personal behavior, a summarization of important concepts, or a celebration of beliefs worth affirming.

The subdivision of the methods into categories is based on the conviction that it's better for you to ask first, "At this stage of the lesson, *what* do I need to accomplish next?" *then*, "What method do I use next?" That two-step process is not readily apparent when you sit in planning sessions with many experienced teachers. Often you hear statements such as, "I think that it would be well for the class to write a paraphrase of the key verse," not, "We need to crystalize the key verse's content into a principle in their language to make sure they've comprehended it well, so what about doing a paraphrase?" Or, "With this class and this topic, we've got to give them a skit or story to tackle!" not, "Since most of the class members would like this topic even though they have little solid information on it, let's let them discover the nature of the topic in a fun way with a clever skit or some lifelike story to analyze!" Thus, since you are a beginning teacher, you will ask,

"What?" and link that to a methods category, then "Which?" as you choose the best method to accomplish your purpose. Your typical lesson will have a method or two chosen from just one category in both the BEGIN and CONCLUDE phases. However, in the DEVELOP phase you will choose methods from two or even three categories. Thus, the natural flow of the chart is down the BEGIN phase, across the DEVELOP phase from left to right, and down the CONCLUDE phase.

SIMPLIFICATION TECHNIQUE THREE:
Get Them Down Pat.

The "them" you are encouraged to "get down pat" refers to *basic* teaching methods. Most methods books do not discriminate between the beginning and the experienced teacher's needs: they mix methods which are normally used, short, and simple with those rarely used or time consuming or which are complex. **TEACH**NIQUE's methods are easily learned and frequently used in sessions of an hour or less. Thus, you will not waste any of your time by learning them all.

Each teachnique is a specific skill to be mastered. Therefore, two sides of a book page are devoted to each of them. You are encouraged to tear out each method page as you learn it and store them all in a notebook to which you can add other methods that you discover. When you get comfortable with lesson planning, the methods and the flow chart are all you will need to keep.

Method
Phase/category
Time

Definitions

Directions

Design

Examples

Exercises

Report

BEGIN/REVIEW

2-10 minutes
1-3 reporters
No space requirements

A1a

DEFINITIONS

Bringing back what you were sent out to get.

An oral, and/or visual, and/or written presentation by one or more persons on an assigned topic, information search, or interview(s).

A succinct communication of an assignment.

DESIGN

A report can increase perspective on an assignment. Since there are as many ways of seeing an issue as there are class members, it is valuable to the teacher and class to expose those viewpoints. A report serves that function.

A report is a way of increasing responsibility for the learning of the class. In a sense, everyone who communicates to the class "teaches." The reporter's report is part of the teaching.

A report can increase student involvement. It can be made short and simple to encourage the shy person or the person of limited ability. It can demand complex and extensive research to include the skills of the talented.

The report, used as a Review method to begin a session, prepares the class for new learning.

DIRECTIONS

1. Spell it out (explain exactly what you want in each report) in adequate detail so that the desired information is found. In order to do this the teacher should put the assignment in writing, keeping one copy. If the report given is not what the teacher thought was requested, the assignment can be evaluated. Often, the wording of the assignment will be vague. To keep this from happening, tell:

   a. what you want done
   b. where the information can be found
   c. the form of report you want (oral, written, visual)
   d. the length of class time allotted to reporting
   e. when the report is to be given

2. Put a note on your calendar to yourself to check with the reporter to see if there is any trouble and if the report is being done.

3. Make the report an integral part of the lesson. If possible, use some of its information in later learning activities. Refer to it from time to time, using the reporter's name, especially if you summarize.

4. Thank the reporter after the report with appropriate commendation. The verbal or written thank-you can refer to the content and/or the method of presentation.

5. File good examples of written and visual reports as examples for later reporters. Examples are often more assuring than specific written instructions.

6. Offer opportunities to report (a) in private to specific persons who have a special skill or need to be more involved in the class and (b) during the class to members in general when most any member could do the assignment.

15

A1a Report

1. EXAMPLE

Here is an illustration of the visual outline of a report given on a Missionary in the First Century." (See A below.)

I. Paul the Jew

   A. Hebrew
   B. Israelite
   C. Child of Abraham
   D. Pharisee
   E. Jewish thinker

II. Paul the Roman

   A. Significance of
   B. Importance of
   C. Requirements

III. Paul's specific ca

2. EXERCISE

Evaluate report assignments A, B, and C according to the criteria under Directions (#1, a-e) on the previous page. Rewrite those parts which you find inadequate (and compare your corrections with others doing this same exercise).

A. (As the class is leaving) "Say, Martha, would you mind bringing some information on Paul to class? I believe our next unit's on him."

B. (Teacher speaks to the whole class) "I need three volunteers to do three-question interviews of six persons each for next Sunday's class opening. You can do these by telephone and it won't take more than five minutes each. You should be able to come to class ten minutes early so that you can write your results on the charts I'll have prepared. I have the assignments in writing. Who will help the class?"

The written assignment: Thank you for helping us. Please call or talk with a male and a female church member from the age brackets 10-18, 19-retirement, and retired. Get their answers to these questions:

1. With what denominations do you usually associate the term "predestination"?
2. Tell me (slowly) what "predestination" means to you.
3. Has the understanding of predestination, meaning that some people are chosen for salvation and others are not, ever bothered you? If so, how old were you and how did you deal with it?

Remember to get persons of both sexes in each age range specified.

Be sure to introduce yourself and tell why you are asking for this information.

Assure them that no names will be used in our informal survey report and thank them.

Arrive at class ten minutes early so that you can write the results of your interviews on newsprint. In the class you will not be asked to report orally, but members may wish to ask questions.

Call me at _____ if you need help. I'll check with you Thursday to see how your interviews are going.

C. (The teacher talks to Jim before the class starts) "Jim, I admire your ability to condense information. Would you be willing to give a five-to-seven minute summary of our class of next Sunday on the following Sunday? I'll give you the lesson plan for next Sunday and you can sort of sit off to the side and take notes during the class. Your summary should show us how our discussion progressed, points of agreement and disagreement, and any conclusions drawn. I have a piece of poster board and a marker for you. You could outline the main points and refer to them as you talk. Your report would be a very valuable introduction to the lesson a week from Sunday.

16

21 METHODS ON 42 BOOK PAGES

The opposite page explains how the front of each method page is structured. The method name appears in large letters at the top left. On the top right is the method's code number and letters, "A1a." If you haven't done so already, tear out the chart on page 8 and place it beside the opposite page. The capital "A" refers to the opening BEGIN phase, the "1" to the Review category, and the "a" to the first method in that category, *report*. For those who don't like codes, that same information plus other characteristics of the method appears in the upper left-hand corner. The phase name is first, the category second, then the average range of time used in the method. The number of persons needed to do or use the method, and any space, furniture, or seating set-up required, is given last. As you use these methods, you may find that this information needs revising: thus, scratch it out and write down what works for you. This is a workbook and you are encouraged to work *on* and *in* it!

The bulk of the front of a teachnique page is devoted to the three D's: Definitions, Design, and Directions, as you see on the opposite page. However, "reading about" is not the same as "learning to do" a method. Therefore, on the back of each teachnique page, we go the second and third biblical mile. The "Examples" show you what the method looks like as a teacher would use it in a lesson. The *report* has the actual outline that a reporter would use, *sequence making* has examples of two types of sequence-making exercises, etc. Just as a picture is worth a thousand words, so examples also make Definitions, Design, and Directions, come alive.

"Exercises," however, are the critical step. You learn to use the method by practicing it, preferably under guidance. You only experience its possibilities when you try it out, ideally with others who are learning to be teachers. Not only are other beginners good guinea pigs, but they can give you feedback—and you can do the same for them. Thus, I hope that **TEACH**NIQUES will be used in classes for new teachers of youth and adults. This is the lowest-threat/highest-yield way to learn how to teach. And it's fun!

When you gather together with other Christians preparing to teach, remind each other that God, the Holy Spirit, is your ultimate Teacher, Strengthener, and Guide. It was God who inspired these words for you to take to heart:

> And his gifts were that some should be apostles, some prophets, some evangelists, some pastors and teachers, to equip the saints for the work of ministry, for building up the body of Christ.
>
> Ephesians 4: 11–12

HOW TO
begin where your pupils are

If your group has interest and knowledge about the topic use

REVIEW METHODS

If your group has interest in but no knowledge about the topic use

DISCOVERY METHODS

If your group interest is low use

MOTIVATIONAL METHODS

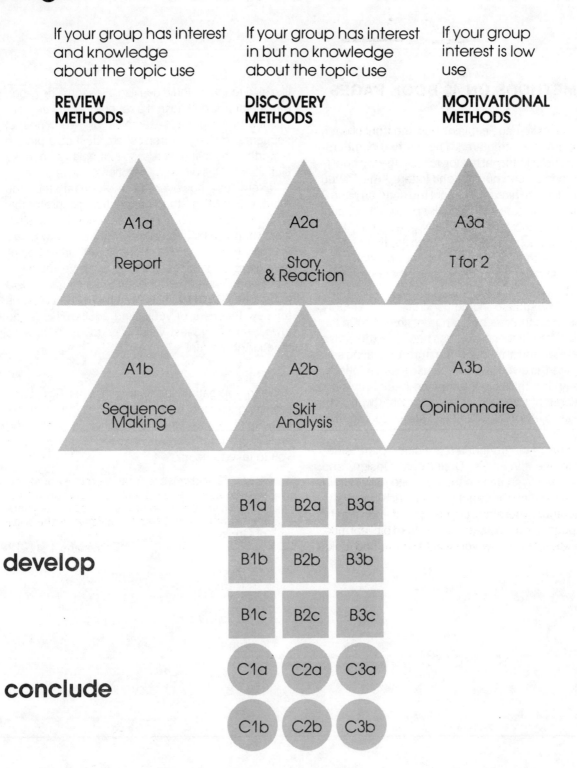

A1a

Report

A2a

Story & Reaction

A3a

T for 2

A1b

Sequence Making

A2b

Skit Analysis

A3b

Opinionnaire

develop

B1a B2a B3a

B1b B2b B3b

B1c B2c B3c

conclude

C1a C2a C3a

C1b C2b C3b

12

begin
where your pupils are

A

One golden rule of teaching is, "start where your pupils are." That's often an impossible ideal because students have different amounts of knowledge about virtually any topic. Have you ever made one of these statements after a class: "My goodness, there wasn't one thing in that whole session that I hadn't heard a dozen times over. How frustrating!"? Or, "Ninety percent of that class was over my head: I wasn't familiar with the key words, the teacher encouraged me to discuss things I knew almost nothing about, and worst of all everyone seemed to think that I ought to know what was going on. How frustrating!"? A good teacher will try to stretch without overwhelming the class members.

As students have different amounts of knowledge about topics, so they also have different degrees of interest in them. Youth may give the teacher more immediate and direct reactions about their likes and dislikes, but there isn't much difference between the adult who nods off to sleep and the teen-ager who gives the thumbs-down signal to a classmate. Yet, first reactions to a topic are often inaccurate. We've all said and heard others say, "That was a good class. I didn't think I was going to enjoy it at first, but you convinced me or got my attention or something. Thanks!" Motivating a class is a challenge, but not an impossible one, especially if the teacher considers motivation when choosing that first method of a class session.

To summarize: good teachers begin their lessons by taking into consideration the degree of knowledge and interest the class has about a topic. The disquieting assumption about that summary is that *all* members of any class do not have the same degree of knowledge about or interest in any topic. However, in and of itself, that is not as great a problem as it seems for two reasons. (1) Most classes tend to be homogeneous. Research indicates that groups become groups because of the alikeness of their members. (2) Groups seem to sense if a method is on target for the group as a whole. Pupils who are behind will try to catch up and those who are ahead will pitch in to help rather than hinder the teacher's efforts. That's the way it should be in the Christian community. As an added bonus, **TEACHNIQUES** gives you a choice of six different methods

to begin the lesson with. The variety in opening methods will also encourage the class to respond positively.

Examine the chart on the opposite page. It is designed to enable you to select the most effective opening method(s) for a lesson. Normally, you'd choose one (sometimes two) method from a category and move on to consider the three DEVELOP categories. The three BEGIN categories face the knowledge-interest challenge: Review methods are for classes which have both interest and knowledge; Discovery methods are for classes which you expect to be interested in a topic that is new to them; and, Motivational methods are for classes where you want to be sure that interest is stimulated immediately in the topic. Let's look at these in some detail.

REVIEW Methods

Most church school lessons and much group study is done in units or series because so many topics need several or many sessions to cover them well. Thus, the most common opening activity connects the class with what it has learned previously so that more can be built on that foundation. Review methods are helpful, in addition, because some people may have missed the previous session or two. This is the teacher's way of saying, "Here is an opportunity for you to catch up."

The *report* is classified as a Review teachnique because it often includes what has been studied or bridges a past lesson with new information for that particular lesson. *Sequence making* is the second Review teachnique. It's offered to you because so much of what we learn, especially in a unit, is sequential, with the class expected to know the whole succession of events or concepts by the completion of the unit. For instance, Christianity is a historical religion; its events happened at different places in time. Thus, to understand our faith you must know our historical heritage. Or, since the Christian life is a faith pilgrimage, Christians share their experiences as a series of events through which God worked in their lives. Therefore, the nature of our faith, historical and personal, justifies *sequence making* as a useful method with which to begin.

DISCOVERY Methods

These teachniques are especially useful when the teacher believes that the topic is new to the class and that the class will enjoy it. They are called "Discovery" methods because they do not just give the topic or principles away but let the class members perceive it for themselves, a much more satisfying educational experience. These methods can be used when a new phase of a unit or series is presented, when a series begins, or with a topic covered in a single session.

Story and reaction presents the class with a situation to which they are to respond. Classes are familiar with having stories told to them by friends, on TV, in sermons. These are chosen to focus their attention on the beginning point of the lesson. *Skit analysis* is similar. These dramatic scenes are chosen or constructed to introduce the lesson content in an even more lifelike context.

MOTIVATIONAL Methods

The underlying principle in this category of teachniques is that they motivate by getting the class members emotionally involved in the topic. In *T for 2,* pairs of class members are asked to argue or dispute a topic from two opposite perspectives. The *opinionnaire* requires that each class member take a series of written stands about a topic. Though each person's opinions are kept secret, the range of class opinions is displayed so that each member can see how his or her opinion compares with the whole group's. These methods offer 100% involvement with very little threat. They are stimulating and practical—and nobody can sleep through them!

And in Conclusion . . .

The classification of these six methods into three categories is not as neat as it appears. As you may have judged, some methods may fit into more than one category. Occasionally you may choose methods from two BEGIN categories to open your class. It is helpful, however, to start with a pattern for the normal and typical use of the methods.

The **TEACH**NIQUES pages are removable so that you can practice each method in a teacher training class. You may not always select the perfect method to begin a session, and you may not always use it perfectly, but your class will appreciate both the variety and the fact that you care enough to try to "start where they are."

Report

BEGIN/REVIEW

2-10 minutes
1-3 reporters
No space requirements

A1a

DEFINITIONS

Bringing back what you were sent out to get.

An oral, and/or visual, and/or written presentation by one or more persons on an assigned topic, information search, or interview(s).

A succinct communication of an assignment.

DESIGN

A report can increase perspective on an assignment. Since there are as many ways of seeing an issue as there are class members, it is valuable to the teacher and class to expose those viewpoints. A report serves that function.

A report is a way of increasing responsibility for the learning of the class. In a sense, everyone who communicates to the class "teaches." The reporter's report is part of the teaching.

A report can increase student involvement. It can be made short and simple to encourage the shy person or the person of limited ability. It can demand complex and extensive research to include the skills of the talented.

The report, used as a Review method to begin a session, prepares the class for new learning.

DIRECTIONS

1. Spell it out (explain exactly what you want in each report) in adequate detail so that the desired information is found. In order to do this the teacher should put the assignment in writing, keeping one copy. If the report given is not what the teacher thought was requested, the assignment can be evaluated. Often, the wording of the assignment will be vague. To keep this from happening, tell:

   a. what you want done
   b. where the information can be found
   c. the form of report you want (oral, written, visual)
   d. the length of class time allotted to reporting
   e. when the report is to be given

2. Put a note on your calendar to yourself to check with the reporter to see if there is any trouble and if the report is being done.

3. Make the report an integral part of the lesson. If possible, use some of its information in later learning activities. Refer to it from time to time, using the reporter's name, especially if you summarize.

4. Thank the reporter after the report with appropriate commendation. The verbal or written thank-you can refer to the content and/or the method of presentation.

5. File good examples of written and visual reports as examples for later reporters. Examples are often more assuring than specific written instructions.

6. Offer opportunities to report (a) in private to specific persons who have a special skill or need to be more involved in the class and (b) during the class to members in general when most any member could do the assignment.

A1a Report

1. EXAMPLE

Here is an illustration of the visual outline of a report given on "The Qualifications of Paul to Be a Missionary in the First Century." (See A below.)

I. Paul the Jew

    A. Hebrew
    B. Israelite
    C. Child of Abraham
    D. Pharisee
    E. Jewish thinker

II. Paul the Roman citizen

    A. Significance of Roman citizenship
    B. Importance of his home town, Tarsus
    C. Requirements of the best Hellenistic education

III. Paul's specific call to the Gentiles

2. EXERCISE

Evaluate report assignments A, B, and C according to the criteria under Directions (#1, a–e) on the previous page. Rewrite those parts which you find inadequate (and compare your corrections with others doing this same exercise).

A. (As the class is leaving) "Say, Martha, would you mind bringing some information on Paul to class? I believe our next unit's on him."

B. (Teacher speaks to the whole class) "I need three volunteers to do three-question interviews of six persons each for next Sunday's class opening. You can do these by telephone and it won't take more than five minutes each. You should be able to come to class ten minutes early so that you can write your results on the charts I'll have prepared. I have the assignments in writing. Who will help the class?"

The written assignment: Thank you for helping us. Please call or talk with a male and a female church member from the age brackets 10–18, 19-retirement, and retired. Get their answers to these questions:

1. With what denominations do you usually associate the term "predestination"?
2. Tell me (slowly) what "predestination" means to you.
3. Has the understanding of predestination, meaning that some people are chosen for salvation and others are not, ever bothered you? If so, how old were you and how did you deal with it?

Remember to get persons of both sexes in each age range specified.

Be sure to introduce yourself and tell why you are asking for this information.

Assure them that no names will be used in our informal survey report and thank them.

Arrive at class ten minutes early so that you can write the results of your interviews on newsprint. In the class you will not be asked to report orally, but members may wish to ask questions.

Call me at _____ if you need help. I'll check with you Thursday to see how your interviews are going.

C. (The teacher talks to Jim before the class starts) "Jim, I admire your ability to condense information. Would you be willing to give a five-to-seven minute summary of our class of next Sunday on the following Sunday? I'll give you the lesson plan for next Sunday and you can sort of sit off to the side and take notes during the class. Your summary should show us how our discussion progressed, points of agreement and disagreement, and any conclusions drawn. I have a piece of poster board and a marker for you. You could outline the main points and refer to them as you talk. Your report would be a very valuable introduction to the lesson a week from Sunday.

Sequence Making

BEGIN/REVIEW

2-10 minutes
Any number of persons
No space requirements

DEFINITIONS

Putting given or recalled facts in an order.

The placement of linearly related facts in a natural or arbitrarily agreed-upon arrangement.

DESIGN

Sequence making is an interesting method because it efficiently groups a large amount of related facts as they are recalled.

Sequence making is a method which can be varied easily. It can be done by individuals, small groups, or the whole group.

Sequence making promotes a mind "set" for new learning because it gives the larger framework in which to put or from which to add new knowledge.

Sequence making is a way to raise forgotten information to consciousness. Recalled information, by association, stimulates the remembering of what appeared to be forgotten facts.

DIRECTIONS

1. Determine if the information given or to be recalled can be put into a sequence or order. Some bases for ordering are:

a. *time:* historical events

b. *consequence:* when a result follows a cause

c. *set order:* such as the sequence of books in the Protestant Bible, the Ten Commandments, etc.

d. *distance:* knowing the relative distance of cities is one means of picturing geographical relationships; such a sequence is found in the Great Commission of Acts 1:8.

e. *successions:* such as kings, prophets, kingdoms, rulers of Israel, ages, etc.

2. Put the information in the desired sequence, and then mix it up by listing the items in alphabetical order. This is how they will be given to the class.

3. Write out carefully worded instructions. To check on the clarity of your instructions, try them out on several people. Since this is often the first activity of a session, it is critical that the directions for putting the facts in sequence be perfect to get off to a strong, smooth start.

4. Decide if you will need to illustrate what you are asking the class to do. If it is necessary (you will often find this out when you try it out on people in a "dry run"), work out a very clear parallel illustration for the class.

5. If you will need special materials such as newsprint, markers, twine and safety pins for a time line, etc., be sure that you have them.

A1b Sequence Making

1. EXAMPLE: Time Sequence (preparation for the study of David's reign)

Instructions: Mark these "1st," "2nd," "3rd," etc., in historical order. Bonus for approximate dates.

_____ First Passover   _____ Philistines take most of Israel   _____ Moses' death

_____ Jericho taken   _____ Promised land settled   _____ Saul is crowned

Ways of doing this activity:

1. Put the six events on the board and (a) ask each individual to write them in order on a piece of paper, (b) have pairs or small groups put them in sequence, or (c) order them by class discussion.
2. Each of these six items can be put on a card and, as the class or each group selects a sequence, they can be taped in place. Children often use clothespins or safety pins to pin the cards to a heavy string, like clothes on a line.

---

2. EXAMPLE: Consequences (a review of the life of John the Baptist)

Instructions: Fill in the blanks from memory or by reading the passages listed below this exercise.

                 Action   Consequence

1. John the Baptist came to prepare the world for _____ .

2. When Jesus presented himself for baptism, John's reaction was _____ .

3. The Old Testament implies that _____ would return in the person of John.

4. John's rebuke of Herod's _____ led to John's being _____ .

5. John said that he must decrease so that Jesus might _____ .

6. When John asked proof of messiahship, Jesus pointed to the _____ he did.

7. As a favor to _____ John was executed.

NOTE: This kind of information is easily obtained from a Bible dictionary, the most important reference book for a teacher. For answers, see (1) Mal. 3:1 and Luke 3:16; (2) Matt. 3:13–15; (3) Mal. 4:5–6; (4) Matt. 14:1–5 and Luke 3:18–20; (5) John 3:25–30; (6) Luke 7:22; and (7) Matt. 14:1–12.

---

3. EXERCISE: Naming the Ten Commandments in Order

Following the Directions on the previous page, write out the complete directions for a set-order sequence activity for the Ten Commandments. Decide whether you wish to give the class just the task, the Bible passage, a list of the commandments in short form ("don't steal") perhaps with wrong additions ("don't hate"), etc. Some find it meaningful to divide the ten into two tables with Table 1 entitled "Our Relationship to God" (commandments 1–4 or 1–5) and Table 2, "Our Relationship to Each Other" (5 or 6–10). Try this teachnique out on several others to be sure it's easily and accurately understood.

NOTE: The Ten Commandments are found in Exodus 20. Verse 3 is #1, 4–6 is #2, 7 is #3, 8–11 is #4, 12 is #5, 13 is #6, 14 is #7, 15 is #8, 16 is #9, and 17 is #10 in most of Protestantism.

4. EXERCISE: The Succession of Kings

The kings came in this historical order: Abimelech (attempted), Saul, David, Solomon, and then the kingdom divides with Rehoboam ruling Judah and Jeroboam ruling Israel. Create an interesting succession activity to get not only the order but which ruled the united and the divided kingdoms. Again, field test it on others to get any confusion out of your directions.

Story & Reaction

BEGIN/ DISCOVERY

5-12 minutes
Any number of persons
No space requirements

A2a

DEFINITIONS

A story is presented which introduces a point or the point of the lesson. The group reacts to it.

A story is told, read, or given in printed form, and the group responds to it according to instructions in order to introduce the group to a topic on which they have little information or experience.

DESIGN

A story, like a riddle, has a point which individuals and groups enjoy discovering.

A story is one good way to begin a session because it gets the group intellectually and emotionally involved in the topic at the outset.

Story presentation with specified reaction psychologically sets the group for learning the main concern or one of the concepts in a topic about which it is relatively ignorant.

Story and reaction is a part of Christian development. Our lives are our stories, and how we react to what happens to us determines our next steps.

Story and reaction is a part of the ministry of Christian support and counsel. We share our "stories" with each other in order to gain the strength which comes from such interactions.

DIRECTIONS

1. Put the issue, problem, circumstance, etc., that you want the class to focus on in a written statement which begins, "The point which I'd like the group to discover from this story is . . ."

2. Select or create a story* which makes that point or a very similar one.

3. Decide how to present the story to the group. You or someone else can tell or read it. Another way is to have the story duplicated and pass it out for individual or group use.

4. Decide *how* the group is to react to the story and *when* you will give them the instructions for that reaction (before or after the story presentation).

5. Decide whether you will apply the story reaction to the topic immediately or ask the group to put the principle or other learnings from the story on "hold" for later use in the session.

*The word "story" here includes what we call "anecdote," "fable," "allegory," "tale," etc. The parables and illustrations which tell of an event or connected happenings which "hang together" would also be included. Church curriculum literature and teacher aid books provide them, and there are many books of nothing but "stories."

A2a Story & Reaction

1. EXAMPLE

Here is an adapted Grimm story used to begin a session on the commandment, "Honor your father and mother."

Many years ago in eastern Europe there lived a poor peasant family. Each evening, after the long day's work was done, they would gather around the table for a simple supper. There were the father and mother, a small boy—the apple of the parents' eye—and an aged, infirm grandfather.

One evening the grandfather spilled some food at the table. "We can't have this!" shouted the mother. "You'll have to eat elsewhere." And so, the next evening the old man sat on a low, three-legged stool in the corner and ate from a heavy, chipped bowl.

Some weeks later the old gentleman was ill and he dropped the bowl while eating. It broke into a thousand pieces! This angered the mother who raged, "If you're going to act like a pig, you'll be fed like one." From that time on the grandfather ate from a small trough while the family ate at the table in front of the cheerful fire.

The next evening, when the father came in from the fields, he noticed his son busily working with hammer, nails, and pieces of wood. With a note of pride in his voice he said, "And what is my young carpenter building tonight?" The lad replied, "Oh, I'm making a trough, Dad, to feed you and Mom out of when you get old."

The mother and father looked at each other, at the old man already in the corner ready for supper, and at the boy. An unspoken decision was made in that moment. They invited the grandfather back to the table, and that's where he stayed—in the family circle.

(The class may be divided into groups or pairs, or these questions may be used for an all-group discussion on the fifth commandment.)

A. What is right about that story for (1) exslaves in the desert with Moses, (2) peasants, and (3) us today? Give evidence.

B. What's wrong or inadequate about the ethical point? Support your critique using ideas expressed in scripture.

2. EXERCISE on 2 Samuel 11 and 12: Nathan's Story

A. Outline Nathan's story and state each parallel in David's sin.

B. What made David angry about this story in his role as (1) chief justice in Israel, (2) receiver of God's message through the prophet, and (3) a human being?

C. Guess at the various excuses and rationalizations David employed which enabled him to ignore his sin up until then.

D. Complete: "Good stories bypass our defenses and excuses by . . ."

3. EXERCISE

With what objective, scripture, or doctrinal point might you use this story? See how many different uses you can find.

A priest was walking among the workmen who were busily working on the construction of a cathedral. He asked each craftsman the same question: "What are you doing?" He got these answers: "I'm laying block." "I'm supporting my family." "I'm helping to build a great cathedral."

Design questions to be given the group before the story—"things to look for." Develop a brief discussion guide to use as you guide the reaction to the story.

Skit Analysis

BEGIN/ DISCOVERY

5-15 minutes
Any number of persons
Room set up so that all can see skit

A2b

DEFINITIONS

A brief, acted-out scene, often humorous.

An acted-out scene (with script memorized or read) which takes little or no preparation to do and still makes the point.

DESIGN

A skit challenges the class to discover its meaning. Being acted out, the skit is more fun than the story, but its results are more variable because the teacher has less control over the content.

Skits require both knowledge and analytical ability. Since they are short, it is assumed that the audience knows something about the issues raised by them. Since skits are lifelike they presuppose the ability to analyze the conflict, issue, resolution, etc.

Natural curiosity is tapped by a skit. People like to guess how it *will, might,* or *should* end.

A skit arouses interest especially if the players present it without having read it in advance. Thus, neither those acting nor those watching know what's going to happen, and that knowledge heightens interest.

DIRECTIONS

1. Choose the concept with which you wish to open the session. Write out a statement of the concept to make sure it is clear in your thinking.

2. You may be able to find a prepared skit which focuses on your concept or is close enough so that you can adapt it easily. Dorcas D. Shaner's *Short Dramas for the Church* (Judson Press, 1980), a book of short "stingers," is an excellent resource for skits and skit ideas which have a bite.

3. You may have to write out a brief skit yourself. Decide if your opening concept could be better discussed through the use of a complete or open-ended skit. A "complete" skit is one in which the scene thoroughly presents the point, exposes or resolves a conflict, or gives various sides in a disagreement. An "open-ended" skit is one which lacks a conclusion, solution, or resolution. It permits the observers to guess how it might have come out, try out different ways of completing the incident, decide on the next best step for one or more of the players to take, etc.

4. Decide whether or not to permit players to practice the skit. If they practice it, decide whether or not they should use scripts.

5. Structure the response to the skit. You may wish to give audience groups "things to watch for," "player's roles to analyze or criticize," discussion questions to use after the skit is presented.

6. After the session, reflect on the skit's effect. This will enable you to improve the speed of preparation and quality of skits you write later.

1. EXAMPLE: Compared to What? (Romans 8:18)

Mary: Hello, Mom. How are things at home?

Mom: They're fine, dear. We had onions from your father's garden, I finished my painting, and no one's had the flu.

Mary: I'm glad to hear that, because I wanted to see how you'd deal with a problem. Let's say you had a daughter in college and she decided to take a . . . leave of absence . . . to be treated for a disease she'd picked up . . . while living with a person of the opposite sex . . . to whom she wasn't married . . . who had just joined the foreign legion. . . .

Mom: My goodness, gracious! Are you sure that—what I mean to say is . . . how could you . . . or she . . . or . . . let me get my breath—this is terrible! (Cries a bit.)

Mary: While you're getting control of yourself let me get your reaction to another problem. What if you had a daughter who got a "D" in chemistry for midterms?

Mom: Well, that's so simple by comparison . . . I'd just say that I knew she was doing her best and to hire a tutor if she thought it'd help.

Mary: Well, I knew that you would see it my way.

2. EXERCISE using a book of skits

Get a copy of one of the volumes of *Discussion Starters for Youth Groups* by Ann Billups (Valley Forge: Judson Press), or *Short Dramas for the Church,* and select several starters/stingers.

a. Put in written statement form the point or principle made or implied in each of your selected skits.

b. Decide, with at least one skit, what you'd like the audience to look for, and plan how you'd use their conclusion after the skit.

c. On at least one other skit, write out the questions you'd use in the follow-up discussion.

3. EXERCISE with curriculum materials

a. Get some curriculum material with lessons which could begin with skits.

b. Practice this skill by writing a skit, either complete or open-ended. If you are working with others, try out each other's skits and see if you can guess the point of others' skits.

c. Again, you may wish to prepare questions or things-to-look-for with your skits.

4. EXERCISE on the conference in Jerusalem (Acts 15)

a. Study this passage with the aid of a good commentary.

b. Put it into open-ended skit form (stop before verse 19) and write out a discussion guide (a list of questions) for the skit follow-up.

c. Another way to use this passage is to make two endings:

(1) One will follow the biblical account which indicates that Gentiles *do not* have to become Jews before they can become Christians.

(2) The other ending should state that Gentiles must become Jews in order to then become Christians.

Do enough research to be able to build into your skits some of the important results each decision would have meant for the church.

d. Write some good questions to follow up both of these endings.

T for 2*

BEGIN/MOTIVATIONAL

5-15 minutes
Pairs of persons
Room for pairs to face each other

A3a

DEFINITIONS

When groups of two persons role-play a moral or religious conflict.

A simulated value conflict between two's in which one challenges and the other defends from a Christian viewpoint.

DESIGN

T for 2 is a kind of contest in which one person is assigned the attack role and the other is given the defensive role in a value conflict. Even though their conflict is played or acted, the students tend to get emotionally involved in the issue—that is, motivated.

Research supports the view that the more lifelike the educational experience, the greater carry-over into life. Value conflicts are situations of significant witness, good or bad. Therefore, increasing our awareness of the way we witness is a growth opportunity for Christians. It is also one of the most practical educational exercises.

Some Christians consider even a simulated attack on our faith or ethics sacrilegious. T for 2 is not for them. However, the church has always developed the discipline of defending (making a case for) the faith; it's technical name is "Apologetics."

DIRECTIONS

1. Since this method is suggested for groups which may lack enthusiasm about a topic, the topic must have an aspect which can be defended and challenged by the group members.

2. Sketch out the T for 2 situation:

   a. Who are the participants and what is the specific point of conflict?

   b. Consider suggesting a line of attack or argument against Christian values.

   c. Consider suggesting a line of defense for Christian values.

3. Decide on the total plan to begin the lessons. These are some things which need to be considered:

   a. How will the group pair off?

   b. Will you assign the attack and defensive positions or will you let them decide?

   c. How much time will you devote to the exercise? Will you tell the pairs how much time they have, or will you just "call" time when it is up?

   d. Will you have "observers" (listeners)? If so, will there be one or two per pair? What will they listen for?

   e. Will you do more than one interaction? For instance, will you ask the two's to reverse roles or let the two observers try the conflicting roles?

   f. What will be the next step after the interaction? Will you analyze the arguments, just move on, or have a general discussion about the content and emotions aroused?

*T = Trouble

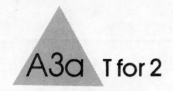

1. EXAMPLE: Cult Weekend

The teacher, knowing that there are 28 members in the class, has them number off in 7's and then the 1's, 2's, etc., form small groups. They letter off in these small groups, A-B-C-D, with "A" having the most recent birthday, "B" the next most recent, etc. The teacher then says:

A and B are married and their 19-year-old child has asked for permission to attend a weekend retreat of the "Love the World for Jesus" family. Parent A believes that youth should make and live with their decisions whereas parent B believes that serious decisions should be reserved to parents and that this is "serious." Argue these points of view for 5 minutes with C listing A's arguments and D listing B's. Go!

When the time is up, the teacher instructs the C's and D's to share their findings with those whose arguments they've analyzed. After 4 minutes for this, the small groups are asked to decide (1) how they were defining "cult" and (2) on what basis a parent should let youth make decisions. These points become the basis of class discussion.

2. EXERCISE: Analyze Example

a. Is this a good topic for a T for 2? Why?

b. What are the advantages and disadvantages of assigning parts by random selection? Would the teacher's choosing-and-grouping be better? What about letting class members group themselves?

c. Would classes know enough about this kind of conflict to be able to role-play it?

d. Is the point of conflict focused clearly enough?

e. Are the time allotments appropriate?

f. Would it be wise for the observers to try out the role play also?

g. Is there a Christian position to defend here?

3. EXERCISE

List as many topics as you can in five minutes that would be good ones for T for 2. Select the best one(s) and write out complete directions. Evaluate your creations according to the criteria in Exercise 2; then try them out with a group.

Opinionnaire

BEGIN/MOTIVATIONAL

1-5 minutes
Any number of persons
No space requirements

A3b

DEFINITIONS

A form used to express one's views about some topic or topics.

A form to be filled out by checking (identifying) statements most like one's views.

DESIGN

An opinionnaire is a method of getting students emotionally involved in a topic because people tend to defend their opinions. Opinion-defense causes motivation.

The anguish of decision making when filling out a well-constructed opinionnaire focuses the students' attention on the importance of the topic for their lives. The topic becomes relevant as well as emotion-laden.

An opinionnaire is an interesting way to introduce some of the complexity of what appears to be a relatively simple topic or issue.

The items on an opinionnaire can reflect the different issues faced in a lesson. In doing this they "set" the mind of the learner to encounter these issues.

An opinionnaire is one of the most efficient means (uses little class time) of securing a large amount of information in a form which is easy to tabulate and report.

DIRECTIONS

1. Jot down the subtopics in the lesson and decide if there could be a variety of opinions about some of them. Matters of *fact* are *not* appropriate.

2. Decide the *form* of opinionnaire you will use. The three types suggested here differ as to how they are answered:

Type 1 (Yes/No)

___ Yes ___ No ___ Don't Know

Type 2 (Degree of agreement)

Strongly Agree	Agree	Undecided	Disagree	Strongly Disagree
_____	_____	_____	_____	_____

Type 3 (By exact expression)

I believe that:
___ Bible reading and the Lord's Prayer should be used in public schools.

___ Bible reading should be used in public schools.

___ Neither should be used in the public schools.

___ I have no set opinion.

NOTE: Open-ended questions are *not* suggested because they take up too much time (e.g., "In regard to Bible reading in the schools, I believe that _____").

3. Determine how the opinionnaire will be presented. The ideal way is to have a printed form for the pupil to fill out. You will have to plan ahead if you want to mimeograph them. Photo duplication is quicker but more expensive. Another way is to put the items on a chalkboard or large piece of newsprint.

4. Choose an efficient method of collecting the information. You may wish to have the pupils report their answers by raising their hands (while their eyes are closed in order to keep people from being influenced by others). Another way is to have printed forms turned in and have an assistant tabulate the results for use later in the lesson. When doing this, it is best to have a tear-off set of answers to turn in so that the pupils can keep the items and their answers to check themselves. (See Example 1 of a Type 1 Opinionnaire.)

5. Design a clearly understood chart for reporting the results. This can be on a prepared piece of newsprint or on a chalkboard.

1. EXAMPLE: Type 1 Opinionnaire

An Opinionnaire on Denominational Pronouncements

Instructions: Mark your opinion about each item *twice;* once after the item and a second time in the left margin. After you have marked all items, tear off the left margin turn-in form. DO NOT put your name on either portion of the opinionnaire.

IN MY OPINION, DENOMINATIONS SHOULD TAKE A STATED POSITION ON THESE ISSUES:

a. Yes ___ No ___ ? ___	a. Gambling (legalized)	Yes ___ No ___ No opinion ___
b. Yes ___ No ___ ? ___	b. Use and availability of alcoholic beverages	Yes ___ No ___ No opinion ___
c. Yes ___ No ___ ? ___	c. Sunday Blue Laws	Yes ___ No ___ No opinion ___
d. Yes ___ No ___ ? ___	d. Abortion	Yes ___ No ___ No opinion ___
e. Yes ___ No ___ ? ___	e. Right to Work Laws	Yes ___ No ___ No opinion ___

2. EXAMPLE: Type 2 Opinionnaire

My Opinion About Ecumenical Cooperation in Our Town: A Checklist

IN MY OPINION, ALL CHURCHES SHOULD:	Strongly Agree	Agree	Undecided	Disagree	Strongly Disagree
a. Hold a joint Thanksgiving service.	___	___	___	___	___
b. Decide fairly which denomination's church is built in each new section of town.	___	___	___	___	___
c. Jointly sponsor a chaplain for the hospital and prison.	___	___	___	___	___
d. Jointly survey the town to find each resident's religious preference.	___	___	___	___	___
e. Encourage their youth to collect money for UNICEF on Halloween.	___	___	___	___	___

3. EXAMPLE: Type 3 Opinionnaire

Your Opinion, Please, About Pilgrimages!

a. A trip to the Holy Land would be:
___ an unparalleled spiritual experience.
___ good religious education.
___ of no special religious significance.

b. Taking your children to visit the place of your birth:
___ helps both parent and child know who they are.
___ helps the parent more than the child in identity formation.
___ helps the child more than the parent in identity formation.
___ helps some persons form their identity.
___ is of no special help in identity formation.

c. A visit to denominational headquarters by a church youth group:
___ aids in the development of religious identity for all.
___ can aid in the development of religious identity for some.
___ is of no special importance in developing religious identity.
___ would bore church kids.

4. EXERCISE

Have your group choose a topic and each member make one type of opinionnaire. Criticize each other's opinionnaires in order to (a) remove all vague terms or instructions, (b) be sure that they can be tabulated easily, and (c) certify them "interesting" or "provocative."

5. EXERCISE

Create reporting charts for your opinionnaires.

develop
the lesson
meaningfully

The purpose of the method(s) chosen to open a session is to get the class's attention by beginning where they are. Thus, you have chosen your method(s) on the basis of their knowledge and interest in the topic, you have gotten their attention, and you are now ready to "take them somewhere"—or DEVELOP the lesson, to use this book's terminology.

DEVELOPING is different from BEGINNING the lesson because, instead of using one category of methods, you normally choose methods from two or even all three. Turn to the chart on the following page and read the categories from left to right, the most common order of their use. Since the majority of your time is spent in this middle phase, it should be comforting to know that you have nine methods, most of which take from three to fifteen minutes, to choose from.

Again, what you are trying to teach determines what you ought to do next. Much of our time is spent communicating the *content* of the Bible and our faith. To do that you would choose from the Presentation (B1) methods category. After the content has been put before the class you may wish to teach its meaning, significance, implications, etc. That is accomplished by utilizing methods from the Elaboration (B2) category. Finally, you may want to get the

biblical, moral, or theological principles into a brief, memorable form. The Generalization (B3) category provides three methods to achieve that objective.

As you move from method to method you will need to plan on making smooth transitions. That is, you will need to figure out how to help your class move, physically and mentally, from one method to the next. For instance, if your lesson has a *skit,* followed by a *lecture* and a *discussion,* you could set the chairs in a semicircle if your discussion will be led by the leader in front. However, if you begin with an *opinionnaire,* followed by a *directed reading* and *discussion* in small groups, you'd set up the room in small circles. When you change the seating arrangement, as in moving from *T for 2* to the *lecture,* you should plan for the most efficient way to move the furniture so that the class's train of thought is not lost.

Again, resist the temptation to think that because you have read about these methods and looked over examples of them you know them. You only know how to use them well after you have practiced using them. Thus, as you do the practice exercises, you may find it helpful to put these **TEACH**NIQUES pages in a notebook of "Methods for My Teaching Ministry."

begin

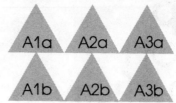

HOW TO
develop the lesson meaningfully

If a body of information is to be communicated use

If the content needs more attention and consideration use

If the content can be developed into a statement or principle use

PRESENTATION METHODS

ELABORATION METHODS

GENERALIZATION METHODS

B1a Lecture	B2a Discussion	B3a Group Definition & Commentary
B1b Interview	B2b Question & Answer	B3b Slogan
B1c Directed Reading	B2c Work Groups	B3c Paraphrase

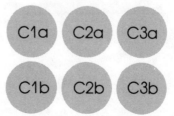

conclude

Lecture

DEVELOP/PRESENTATION

10 or more minutes
Any number of persons
All able to see lecturer

B1a

DEFINITIONS

An organized talk given by a qualified person.

A formal, organized oral presentation delivered by a person competent in the subject or discipline.

DESIGN

A lecture is a very efficient way of communicating information.

A lecture is one of the most used and familiar ways of gaining information, especially in educational settings.

A lecture can bring together the information of specific interest to the group from a far wider range of sources than the listeners could ever explore by reading.

A lecture can bring together information not readily available in commonly published written sources.

A lecture can be followed by many other methods, such as question and answer, discussion, listening teams, audio visuals, etc. These techniques tend to increase the motivation for the listeners to pay attention to and take notes on the lecture.

DIRECTIONS

1. During preparation the lecturer must keep in mind the content to be covered, the level of presentation (popular or scholarly), the time allotted, and the group to be addressed.

2. After mastering the content to be covered, the lecturer must prepare a logical outline with an interesting introduction and meaningful conclusion. ("Meaningful" means an appropriate summary, obvious or implicit applications, or unresolved issues, etc.)

3. The lecture notes should be prepared. Good notes are usually phrases which call to mind specific units of content.

4. The difficult and/or dull points of a lecture may be made more interesting/lucid by the use of illustrations and human interest stories.

5. The visual presentation of the outline of the lecture will make its structure more evident. This can be done in many ways: by giving out a printed sheet with the outline on it (with space to take notes), by having the outline on a poster or chalkboard, or by projecting the outline on a screen using an overhead projector transparency, uncovering each point as it is presented.

6. When the lecturer explains a series of items during the lecture it is helpful to have these projected to focus attention. In Example 1, "Melanie's Lecture Outline," such a series is presented under "III. The significant cases."

B1a Lecture

1. EXAMPLE

Here is Melanie's Lecture Outline on *Church, State, and Public Schools* (see pp. 73–77).

Introduction: Cartoon showing poster at public school: "In case of atomic attack, do not pray until you leave school. It's illegal here!" Why?

I. Why the first amendment was written (1791)
  A. European precedent
  B. The Colonial situation

II. The degree to which the amendment was obeyed in the schools
  A. The Protestant bias of the early public schools
  B. The Roman Catholic challenge in New York state
  C. The parochial school response to "godless" (religiously neutral) schools

III. The significant cases
  A. Pierce vs. Sisters, 1924, the right to parochial education
  B. McCullum vs. Illinois, 1948, sectarian religion not to be taught in the schools
  C. Various cases, the rights of schools to cooperate in released-time religious education off school property
  D. Schempp vs. Abingdon Twp., 1963, the illegality of the praying of the Lord's Prayer and the attempt of New York State Regents to prepare an acceptable nonsectarian prayer: "Almighty God, we acknowledge our dependence upon Thee and we beg Thy blessings upon us, our parents, our teachers, and our country." Conclusion: any prayer is sectarian.
  E. The "child-benefit" theory of the Supreme Court and its applications
  F. Religious activities which are acceptable

Conclusion: "Shared time" expresses the court's views because it supports both the parents' and states' rights.

2. EXERCISE

Evaluate these lecture notes according to the criteria given under DIRECTIONS on page 29.

3. EXERCISE for individuals or groups

A. Think of the two best and worst lectures you have heard.

B. Write out the characteristics which caused you to classify the "best" ones best and the "worst" ones worst.

C. Group all these characteristics into a single list with uniformly positive statements. For instance, change "the lecturer stared at the light fixture" to "the lecturer had good eye contact with the audience."

D. Group your statements into several broad categories such as "the content of the lecture," "the body language," "the spoken and visual illustrations," etc.

E. Develop this into a checklist evaluation form that could be used to judge almost any lecture. Use this checklist as a planning form to make sure your lectures are classified by your students as among the "best" ones.

F. Have observers critique your lecture using one of these lecture evaluation forms. This will inform you of your strengths and weaknesses. Also helpful: if you have access to videotape equipment, tape your lectures and use your form to critique yourself.

NOTE: Good teachers are always working to improve one or more of the methods they use. If you lecture a great deal, work to improve your lecturing skills!

Interview

DEVELOP/PRESENTATION

5-15 minutes
Any number of persons
Space to see interviewees

B1b

DEFINITIONS

A formal face-to-face information gathering by one or more persons *from* one or more others.

An interpersonal involvement with the acknowledged purpose of one or more persons eliciting ideas, opinions, beliefs, reactions, etc., from other(s). This may be done in the presence of observers or an audience.

DESIGN

An interview demands little preparation by the experts interviewed but a great deal of preparation by those who do the interviewing.

An interview is an interesting, live way of getting information, attitudes, and opinions. It gives more information than filling out a form because the interviewer (and observers or audience) can see the person(s) answering and gain impressions from body language, voice inflection, etc.

An interview gets information which might not be gained in written or formal spoken communication. Points left vague may be pursued, points of interest may get more attention, ideas triggered by answers may be followed up, and even the intuition of the interviewer can be employed.

DIRECTIONS

1. Decide for good reasons such as these (not that it can take up time or charm the group) that an interview is the best method to use:

   a. The person to be interviewed is an expert.

   b. The topic is hard to explain unless one is an expert.

   c. The interviewee has the confidence of the group.

   d. The information is controversial and the interviewee is able clearly to discriminate one or more of the points of view.

   e. A biblical or historical person will "come alive" if played well in a dramatized interview.

2. When you book the person(s) to be interviewed be sure to give time, place, length of meeting, audience, topic to be discussed, how the interview will be structured (who will ask questions), and, if a group is to be interviewed, who the other persons are. It may be helpful to share with the one(s) to be interviewed information about the class topics which have led to the session. If you're enlisting someone to pretend to be a biblical or historical character, give instructions for preparation.

3. Prepare an interesting *and accurate* introduction for the person(s) interviewed.

4. Prepare a list of questions, each with one or more follow-up questions, that is, different forms of the original question or questions which continue the line of thought by asking for opposing points of view, implications, etc.

5. During the interview, try to make the person interviewed as comfortable as possible. Use your questions but don't be afraid to follow your intuition if the point seems of interest to the group. Try to sense the reactions of the group as well as those of the person interviewed in order to guide the pace of the interview.

6. Be sure to thank the interviewee after the session and later in writing.

B1b Interview

1. EXAMPLE: A Dramatized Interview with Moses, Talk-show Style

NOTE: The example assumes that both "Moses" and the interviewer have done their homework by studying the first four chapters of Exodus and an article on Moses in a Bible dictionary.

Interviewer:

This is Iszekiah of SBC (Sinai Broadcasting Company). Today we have a man with us who believes that his work is to compel Egypt to release its Hebrew slaves and make them into a nation which can conquer Canaan! Please give a cordial welcome to Moses, a man with a big dream!

A. I can tell by your accent that you're not a Sinai native. Tell us about yourself, especially about your escape from death in infancy.

  1. Who are the Hebrews and why are they special?

  2. Couldn't you just be having a mid-life crisis? Didn't your foster parents treat you well?

  3. Show us an image of your God. What is his specialty—war, fertility, good personal fortune? Where does he act—in the hills, deserts, etc.? Who is his consort?

B. Egypt is "the" power in this area. How do you propose to get them to free your fellow Hebrews without a tremendous army? Do you have a plan?

  1. How do you know these Hebrews really want to be free?

  2. How will you get them organized?

  3. Here is a map. What route do you plan to take and how can you avoid the Egyptian military camps along the coastal highway?

C. Moses, this is an overwhelming task. Why not just stay here in Sinai and enjoy the good life with your family?

  1. How does your family feel about this plan?

  2. Is anybody going to help you?

Tie Up: What do you anticipate as your greatest challenges in freeing these slaves and making a nation out of them?

2. EXERCISE

Have the interview presented in Example 1, after the suggested preparation, to gain practice in this technique.

3. EXERCISE

Evaluate the interview presented in Example 1 according to the criteria given in the DIRECTIONS for the interview method. If you try out this interview, evaluate it before and after doing it to see what additional insights can be gained.

4. EXERCISE: Separation of Church and State

In the Example of the lecture outline (B1a) Melanie, an attorney, is going to lecture on the separation of church and state as it applies to the public school. She will deal with all of the issues represented in the opinionnaire, "What's Your Opinion? The Church, the State, and Public Schools," given in Lesson Planning Example #3 in chapter 5. Could the interview method be used for this topic just as well? Explain.

If you conclude that the interview is an appropriate method to introduce this topic, prepare the interview plan you would use with Melanie, the lawyer. Use the material from the lecture outline and opinionnaire mentioned above to prepare questions and follow-up questions according to the form presented in the following example.

Directed Reading

DEVELOP/PRESENTATION

3-10 minutes in class
Any number of persons
No special seating

B1c

DEFINITIONS

Reading with specific purpose in mind.

A short reading assignment to accomplish a task—such as finding something, answering questions, analyzing points of view, etc.

DESIGN

Directed reading implies that the reader will be asked to recite, thus increasing motivation.

Printed material is a very efficient way of presenting information because:

1. experts can teach students through it;

2. people can read faster than others can talk;

3. reading material is distilled and edited to communicate to a level of readership efficiently and interestingly.

Directed reading is more effective than nondirected because there is a "set" or built-in search strategy operating.

DIRECTIONS

1. Select a piece of reading to be done in the session which:

   a. contains a succinct and/or authoritative presentation of the content, such as the Bible, a creed, or denominational pronouncement, and which

   b. is short enough for everyone to read in 2 to 10 minutes.

   NOTE: The longer the reading assignment, the greater the difference in time it will take the fastest and slowest readers. Therefore, when using lengthy pieces, assign reports to small groups. The students will wait on each other and be ready in time for reporting. If you let everyone read individually (especially if there is not "something to look for"), those who finish early are likely to start side conversations. This puts the teacher in the position of "order restorer" and embarrasses those who read slowly.

2. Decide how the class will read the piece if it is not printed in curriculum which is available in the classroom in sufficient quantity for all class members. (Don't assume that lesson books will be brought by all class members to a class.) You may wish to duplicate the material by mimeograph, ditto, or photocopy; *or,* if the piece is quite short, project it from an overhead projector on a screen using a prepared transparency.

3. Determine whether you will give the class "something to look for" when they read the material and whether all will look for the same thing. Write out the instructions and decide whether you will give these to the groups within the class on that same piece of paper or orally. Include in this part of your plan how what has been found will be utilized, *e.g.,* in report groups, by individuals, etc.

4. If you choose to have the class read the material without "something to look for," write out what you will ask the class to ascertain from having read it and determine how you will ask them to respond, which will often move you to one of the Elaboration methods found next in this book.

1. EXAMPLE: Reading Assignment for the Apostle's Creed

a. What persons are included in the creed other than the persons of the Trinity? What is the topic of the paragraph in which they both appear? Why were they chosen?

b. If you could add one other person to this portion of the creed, who would it be? Explain your reason for including that person.

c. Why aren't any people mentioned in the other two paragraphs of the creed, that is, those about the Father and Holy Spirit?

d. If you could add a person to each of these paragraphs, who would they be? Justify your selections.

2. EXAMPLE: A Comparison of the Gospels

Each of the four Gospels was written to present Jesus in a certain way to a specific audience. A clue to these purposes and readers is the person or time with which the writers start their stories. Look up the following verses and, as a group, guess what the author is trying to accomplish with his choice of person and time. You will have ten minutes to work. Jot down your conclusions on this sheet beside the appropriate verses.

Mark 1:4 _____

_____

Matthew 1:2 _____

_____

Luke 3:38 _____

_____

John 1:1, 6 _____

_____

3. EXERCISE: Preparing a Directed Reading Assignment

a. How would you present this passage to the class? Would having different versions and paraphrases available be better than using just one? Should it be read from Bibles, by a reader, put on the board, etc.?

b. What phrases might the readers find difficult to interpret confidently? Where would you get and how would you present that necessary information to them?

c. Do the passages which precede and follow this one help the readers in any way to understand the passage? If so, how would you build that into the directed reading?

d. How would you get your students to analyze the central point of both incidents referred to in the passage?

Write up your complete assignment for small groups including the amount of time you'd allow and how reports would be made.

Discussion
DEVELOP/ELABORATION

3 or more minutes
6-12 persons is best
Circle of chairs is ideal

B2a

DEFINITIONS

The sharing of opinions, ideas, information, attitudes, etc., about a subject by group members.

The organized exploration of a topic by the interaction of group members which is accomplished either by a leader who structures the development of the topic or by the group's self-discipline.

DESIGN

Discussion presents optimum opportunity for the involvement of all of a group's members in productive and nonproductive ways.

Discussion appears to be the least demanding of methods. However, an effective discussion demands three skills:

1. *Self-Discipline*
(Am I talking too much or too little, do my comments address the topic, and are my emotions distinguished from my opinions in what I say?)

2. *Other Awareness*
(Are some members, who want to talk, by-passed by the speed of the discussion? Could I move the discussion beyond the domination of several members by addressing my comments to someone else?)

3. *Discussion Progress Monitoring*
(Are we following the agreed-upon subject outline with adequate time for each major topic? If we've gotten off the topic, should I say so and move the discussion back on the topic?)

DIRECTIONS

1. If you want the group to prepare for the discussion, give instructions as specifically as possible, not only on *what* is to be read, but *questions* to be answered, *reactions* to be given to opinions, *issues* to be analyzed, etc. Thank those who made preparation when the discussion begins.

2. Decide if you want to present an "agenda" or whole discussion outline to the group to begin the session *and* whether or not you wish to get their approval for that agenda.

3. Prepare a series of major questions, each with reserve minor questions designed to develop in depth all major points to be discussed. It should be in outline form.

4. Help the group to discipline itself by calling attention to digressions from the topic, the amount of time and topic remaining, whether all are participating, etc.

5. Decide if you will be an impartial discussion leader or will express your opinions in the discussion. You may wish to inform the group of your "style."

6. Be fair in your summarizations. As you conclude one point and move to the next one, reflect the group's thinking accurately.

7. After the conclusion of the discussion, express specific appreciation if you believe the group has worked hard, been especially sensitive to each other, thought in depth, etc.

35

B2a Discussion

1. EXERCISE:
Observing Interaction in a Discussion

Because it is difficult to participate in a discussion and analyze what is going on at the same time, an observer can help a group to gauge its degree of total membership involvement by the use of a diagram. To do this the observer makes a circle for each member in the diagram representing the seating arrangement. When the first person speaks and the second responds, a line is drawn on the diagram with an arrowhead on that line to indicate the flow of communication, like this:

Ann ————⟶ Ben

The completed chart can be analyzed to find out many things: who spoke how many times, who spoke to whom, which members tended to dominate the discussion, which were left out (or chose to stay out), etc. Usually a ten-minute segment in the middle of a longer discussion is a representative sample with which to try this method of observing interaction. However, be sure to get the permission of the members before you do this analysis. See the Example 2.

2. EXAMPLE: Diagram of the Flow of Communication in a Group Discussion

NOTE: This diagram is quantitative; it gives only the number and directions of the communications. It does not tell how long each person spoke or the quality of what they had to say. Nor does it show if a person's communication was directed at another person, just who responded to what communication.

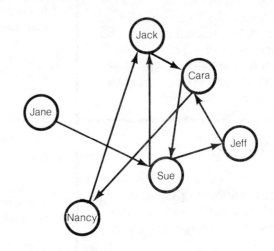

3. EXERCISE

Continue to develop the evaluation form below, which assesses the *quality* of responses, with at least 10 positive and 6 negative categories.*

Instructions: Each time a communication is voiced check the qualities on the form which best characterize it. Use this for a whole discussion or at least 10 minutes of a discussion after it has begun. Present the findings to the group after the discussion to give them insight into their contributions to increase the quality of their efforts.

NOTE: This can be done with a tape recording if each person's voice can be identified. Video taping is also effective. When using a recording, each person can evaluate his/her own comments. That will be less threatening.

	Participant	Jack	Cara	Jeff	Sue	Nancy	Jane
Positive Responses	Gave idea	✓				✓	
	Asked question	✓	✓	✓	✓		✓
	Summarized				✓		
Negative Responses	Got group off topic		✓				
	Interrupted				✓		

*Positive responses: Answered a question, supported a view, volunteered information, challenged a view, gave another view, asked for clarification, shared helpful illustration, helped group discipline itself, etc.

*Negative responses: Tended to be vague, put down someone, ridiculed an idea, distracted, got angry, talked too long, etc.

Question & Answer

DEVELOP/ELABORATION

1-5 minutes
30 persons or less typically
Best if all can see leader and answerer

DEFINITIONS

Where the subject is explored by a series of questions, asked by the teacher, with one or more students answering them.

An inductive method in which students are "led" to conclusions by the use of carefully prepared major and follow-up questions.

DESIGN

Questioning is a method which calls for active rather than passive students.

Questioning gives the teacher feedback at more frequent intervals than most other methods.

Questions can be used for virtually all kinds of learning processes: memorizing, explaining, perceiving relationships, reviewing, applying, appreciating, discriminating, etc.

Questions are one of the most precise ways for pupils to learn areas of full and partial agreement and disagreement.

Questions are a good means of enabling students to discover for themselves, a most satisfying form of creative thinking.

DIRECTIONS

1. Be sure the students have enough information to use the question and answer method to explore the topic or one aspect of it.

2. Write a series of questions which lead, step by step, through the examination of the topic, or one aspect of the topic. All yes/no, either/or questions should include a "why" or further elaboration follow-up.

3. The leader should specify to whom the question is asked: to anyone who wishes to answer it, to a particular person or persons (e.g., "those who haven't spoken up until now"), etc.

4. The leader should wait comfortably for an adequate period of time before the question is paraphrased or an alternate question is asked. When asking questions, count for five seconds ("1,000 and one, 1,000 and two," etc.) before reacting. A questioner's sense of elapsed time is distorted in proportion to his/her anxiety.

5. Deal honestly but supportively with wrong or partially wrong answers. Focus on the concept rather than the person at these points.

6. If you want the members of the group to share in the questioning process, rather than just having a strict leader-to-pupil series of interchanges, structure this interaction with such phrases as: "Who wants to support or challenge this point of view?" "Give your answer to the class instead of me and get them to react to it . . ." (And then, stand to the side or join the group so that the person answering will be the natural focus of the group.)

B2b Question & Answer

1. EXAMPLE:
On the Writing of the Gospels

". . . and so, somewhere between 25 and 40 years after Jesus' ascension, after the first wave of persecution, our first Gospel was written."

a. Why had so many years gone by? (How long did believers think it would be before Jesus returned? See John 21:20-23.)

b. What was it about this period of time that might have caused the early Christians to change their minds about Christ's imminent return? (Assume that the apostles had been born within 10 years of Jesus' birth, and place Mark's writing about A.D. 65.)

c. Nero was the emperor from A.D. 54-68. What is known about the way he treated Christians which may have encouraged Gospel writing? (The placing of the death of the first disciple, James, around A.D. 45 and tradition's teaching that all other disciples except John died as martyrs over the next few decades is a further clue.)

d. The apostles had the authority to settle disputes about what Jesus really did and taught. Since disputes kept cropping up, why would the apostles' aging make the church leaders "nervous"?

2. EXAMPLE/EXERCISE
Extending Discussion

Every teacher needs some stock phrases for extending discussion which are also valuable in the questioning process. Here are some of mine. See if you can add to this list.

a. "Could you illustrate that so that all of us will be sure of what you mean?"

b. "Would you please restate your answer, perhaps in a little longer form, so that everyone can get your position clearly?"

c. "Can you think of other positions on this issue that differ from yours? Would you give one? The contrast will make it clearer for us, I think."

3. EXAMPLE/EXERCISE:
Responses to Imperfect Answers

Many teachers have phrases which they use as basic responses to both partially correct and incorrect answers. They use variations on these phrases depending upon the question content, the person answering, etc. Here are some possible responses. Add to this list responses which reflect your unique way of expressing yourself, and rewrite those from this list to fit your way of talking. Make them "yours."

For wrong responses:

a. "Let's back up and come at this question another way." (Use back-up questions leading to the same point.)

b. "Let's see if this point of view holds up." (Use further questions, showing the point's inadequacy but leading to the truth.)

c. "Who has another answer? Let's get several options out before testing them."

For partially correct answer:

a. "Your answer is basically on solid ground. Let's see if we can make it perfect." (Use questions to isolate and correct error.)

b. (To other class members) "What can you support about this answer and why . . . ? What can we correct?"

c. "(person's name), this is the part of your answer that is on target in my opinion . . . . Why do you think I'm not sure about . . . ?"

4. EXERCISE:
Evaluation of Your Questions

Write out a series of questions on a topic. Have a friend prepare a set on the same topic. Then, try them out on each other. Even though you may know the answers, give some wrong and partially correct answers to provide practice in coping with the "less than perfect." Help one another improve your questions by checking them according to the criteria given in the DIRECTIONS on the previous page.

Work Groups

DEVELOP/ELABORATION

5-20 minutes
6 or more persons
Work space for each work group

B2c

DEFINITIONS

Dividing the education work of the whole group among sub-groupings.

When specific learning tasks are assigned to units of more than one person so that everyone except the leader(s) belongs to a group.

Work groups is not a "pure" method because the groups actually do other methods, such as discussion or report preparation.

DESIGN

Work groups are valuable when there are more subtopics than can be dealt with by the whole group during a session.

Work groups are a means of increasing personal involvement in very large groups.

Permitting each person to volunteer for a work group because of interest in the task/topic increases motivation.

Work groups encourage shy members, who might not speak before the whole group, to express their opinions and to perform small functions such as watching the time or taking notes. In other words, it develops leadership, at beginning levels.

DIRECTIONS

1. Be sure that your reason for using work groups is legitimate; it should not be used just to consume time. Are there more topics than the group as a whole can deal with? Is there a need to get everyone emotionally involved in the topic?

2. Divide the topic into subassignments so that there are enough to keep each group to under eleven persons. It's better to give more than one group the same assignment than to have oversized groups. In *some* situations you may give each small group the same assignment.

3. Decide how you will divide your whole group into work groups: by their choice, randomly, by your choice, by table groups, by skills, etc.

4. Choose a method for securing a leader, reporter, and time watcher for each small group. It saves time to use some random appointment system such as "the person with the next birthday will lead, the one to his/her right is the reporter, and left is the time watcher."

5. A written assignment should be prepared for each group. It should include:

a. what they are to do

b. how many minutes they have to do it

c. if a leader is to be used, how that leader is to be selected (person whose first name is last alphabetically, the group shall decide, the one at the head of each table, etc.)

d. the form in which the group is to report or share

e. if there is a reporter, how that person is selected

f. if resources (Bible reference books, for instance) are necessary, where they are to be obtained.

6. Monitor your small groups while they work to see if they have problems, will finish on time, or need assistance.

1. EXAMPLE: A Work Group Exercise on Magic and Superstition

Resources: Dictionaries, single and multivolume Bible dictionaries

Group A — Choose a general name for what is forbidden in these passages. List and define all the types of this activity that are listed in these passages. Why is there such stern punishment for doing these?

Deuteronomy 18:9–14; Leviticus 19:26, 31; 20:6, 27; and Exodus 22:18.

Group B — What is the New Testament view of the magic arts? Name and define each "art." Why is the New Testament so vehement against these activities?

Acts 13:6–10; Galatians 5:19–21; 2 Timothy 3:8 and its cross reference Exodus 7:11; Revelation 9:21; 18:23; 21:8; and 22:15.

Group C — Is using *chance* to make a decision biblically acceptable? See Acts 1:15–26. Why? In Isaiah 3:1–3 the prophet describes the important occupations and ranks of the deported Jews. What magic-related vocations were there (define each) and why do they appear to be ranked equally with other occupations?

2. EXERCISE

Evaluate the work group assignment at left for the group you will teach using the criteria on the preceding page, especially the points made in DIRECTION #5.

If you find omissions, make additions to improve the assignments.

If you find weaknesses or errors, improve by changing to better wording, verse selection, instructions, etc.

3. EXERCISE: Beatitude Reversal (Matthew 5:3–10)

Take the following devotional exercise and turn it into a work group assignment.

The Beatitudes hardly represent what our dog-eat-dog society teaches us about how to "make it." Fill in the blanks with how you hear the world reversing these sayings.

Stupid are the: poor in spirit, for they shall _____ .

those who mourn, for they shall _____ .

the meek, for they shall _____ .

those who hunger and thirst for righteousness, for they shall be _____ .

the merciful, for they shall _____ .

the pure in heart, for they shall *miss most of the fun* _____ .

the peacemakers, for they shall _____ .

those who are persecuted for righteousness' sake, for they shall be _____ .

Group Definition & Commentary

DEVELOP/GENERALIZATION

5-15 minutes
Any number of persons
Space to work in groups and to present reports

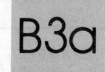

B3a

DEFINITIONS

An exact explanation by a group with a further explanation of that definition (often illustrated).

A precise and complete statement of a concept by a group with elaboration on the meaning, historical context, etc., which makes the definition more meaningful.

DESIGN

Group definition is specified because explaining to others what we mean and agreeing upon definitions and their meaning (1) helps us clarify our concepts and (2) gives us practice in expressing our faith concepts to others.

Definitions are exact, clear statements of the "nature of things." In the case of religious instruction, they are typically concepts, doctrines, and principles.

Commentaries are designed to make definitions "come alive" through the use of explanation and illustrations meaningful to the group.

Definition and commentary are exercises in the precise use of language. It is often difficult to create them because (1) our use of language tends to be informal and (2) we are more conditioned to *learn* (memorize) accepted religious definitions.

DIRECTIONS

1. A definition, in the "generalization" sense of the word, would be appropriate when important concepts need to be remembered with a good degree of clarity. Otherwise, it is not worth the time and frustration of group effort.

2. Select the word or words you wish to be defined.

3. Determine the best size of working groups. In addition, decide if you want more than one group working on each word if you have more than one word. Since some persons are more gifted in working with verbal concepts, you may wish to assign specific people to each small group to get a talent balance. On the other hand, persons may wish to become working groups by their interest in particular words or in working with particular people.

4. Provide specific written instructions for the groups. You may wish to designate the level (for adults, children, etc.) of the definition and commentary or the degree of formality (dictionary, catechism, tract, etc.). Specify who will lead the groups, how long they will have to work, what resource books and materials will be made available, and how the groups will report their results.

5. Determine how the definitions and commentaries will be used by the group in that session or perhaps later in the unit.

6. Since "working with words" can be frustrating, gauge the group's reaction to the method before using it again.

1. EXAMPLE:
The Tongues Spoken at Pentecost

(The Definition and Commentary)

The class had studied Acts 2. They had been asked to generalize and comment on what they learned about tongues from this chapter.

Definition: The tongues spoken at Pentecost are reported as foreign languages, probably spoken with great emotion, as the result of the reception of the Holy Spirit.

Commentary: Verses 8–11 list the known nations of the world to which the disciples would go as missionaries, fulfilling the Great Commission of Jesus to be his witnesses "to the end of the earth."

2. EXAMPLE:
The Tongues Spoken After Pentecost

(The Definition and Commentary)

The class studied 1 Corinthians 14 and other references to tongues in Acts, especially 10:46 and 19:6 in context, after the initial second chapter account.

Definition: The tongues spoken after the day of Pentecost experience are ecstatic sounds, not from any known languages, and are interpretable only by those who have this separate gift.

Commentary: In 1 Corinthians 12:30, Paul clearly discriminates between the gifts of speaking and interpreting tongues. In 1 Corinthians 14:26–28 he limits their use in worship to a maximum of three speakers and only then when there are interpreters present.

3. EXAMPLE:
"You shall not kill." (Exodus 20:13)

(The Assignment, Part I)

Define the word "kill" in this commandment by looking up passages which deal with the subject, such as Genesis 9:5,6; Leviticus 20:16; and Joshua 6:24. Other passages which use the word in a way which defines it may be found by consulting a concordance. A commentary on Exodus should be consulted because "kill" is not a good translation of the Hebrew word. Take ten minutes to write your definition.

(The Assignment, Part II)

Rewrite your definition of "kill" so that it includes your viewpoint on abortion, forms of birth control in which the fertilized ovum is dislodged or the sperm is killed, and the discontinuance of life support systems for a person, most of whose brain functions are gone, etc.—*if* you can agree. You will discover that to define "kill" is to define "life" or "human life" also. Take 15 minutes to prepare your new definition and commentary.

4. EXERCISE:
Writing a Group Definition

Assignments

Study the objectives from curriculum you will use or thumb through a theological wordbook or Bible dictionary for words worthy of definition. Choose a word and write out the assignment. If you do this in a class, exchange papers and check each other's work by the criteria given in DIRECTIONS on the previous page.

Slogan

DEVELOP/GENERALIZATION

5-10 minutes
Any number of persons
Space to work in small groups

DEFINITIONS

A clever phrase or sentence supporting a position.

A succinct statement designed to reflect a principle in a most attractive way.

A compressed viewpoint developed to appeal to a specific group of people.

DESIGN

In order to put a principle into a slogan, the principle itself must be understood. Thus, the slogan is a generalization method because it requires a group to state the principle in order to decide how to package that principle in a slogan.

A "slogan" includes a wide variety of forms, such as the proverb ("Pride goes before destruction . . . ." Proverbs 16:18a), the aphorism ("A stitch in time saves nine."), or those used in advertising, seen on bumper stickers, etc. Thus, it has a wide range of opportunities to appeal to as many people as possible.

Slogans are memorable because of their form but, more important, they enable us to recall the principle behind them.

DIRECTIONS

1. Be sure that the statement of principle is relatively simple and free of numerous exceptions. Complex principles with many exceptions are better done with Definition and Commentary or just stated by the teacher.

2. The first time you use this method you should give examples of slogans with which they are already familiar. Some of these are given in Example 1 on the following page.

3. State the principle in writing yourself and create a few test slogans to be sure that this will be a meaningful and not a frustrating learning experience.

4. Decide how you will have the group create the slogans: as individuals, pairs, small groups, etc.

5. Determine how the slogans will be presented to the group.

6. Determine what the group will do with them. Some options for responding to slogans are presented in Exercise 4 on the next page.

B3b Slogan

1. EXAMPLE:
Slogans Found in the Bible

a. "Let not him that girds on his armor boast himself as he that puts it off."

(1 Kings 20:11)

b. "Let us eat and drink, for tomorrow we die."

(Isaiah 22:13)

c. "The fathers have eaten sour grapes, and the children's teeth are set on edge."

(Jeremiah 31:29 and Ezekiel 18:2)

d. "Like mother, like daughter."

(Ezekiel 16:44)

e. "Like people, like priest."

(Hosea 4:9)

f. "The tree is known by its fruit."

(Matthew 12:33)

g. "Physician, heal yourself."

(Luke 4:23)

h. "Jesus is Lord." (found in many variations)

i. "Maranatha!" ("Our Lord, come!")

(1 Corinthians 16:22)

j. "Whatever a man sows, that he will also reap."

(Galatians 6:7)

2. EXERCISE:
Analyzing Biblical Slogans

Not all of the slogans quoted above express the biblical viewpoint. Often they are quoted to be argued against. Which ones from this list are unbiblical? (See answers upside down below.)

Slogans can be classified as:

Exhortations (encouragement to do something)

Explanations (interpretations of an event)

Affirmations (expressions of belief/truth)

Classify the above into these categories. (See answers upside down below.)

3. EXERCISE

Study the Bible passages and complete the partially written slogans. (Slogan "a." is an illustration.)

a. Forgiven is as forgiven _____ .

(Matthew 6:12)

b. There is no currency devaluation _____

_____ . (Matthew 6:19, 20)

c. Life is an investment in _____

_____ . (Luke 6:22)

d. A person in need is a neighbor _____

_____ . (Luke 10:29–37)

e. Loveless deeds are like _____

_____ . (1 Corinthians 13)

f. It is faith alone which saves, but the faith which saves is _____

_____ . (James 2:14ff.)

4. EXERCISE: Ways to Present Slogans

Creative groups will enjoy and profit by presenting slogans to fellow students, because it will give them an understanding of the powerful informal education which occurs through this form of propaganda. It will also enable them to see that a clever saying is not necessarily true because it's clever—as is illustrated by b. and c. in Example #1. Take the slogans created in #3 or use those in #1 and present them in one of these forms:

Billboard

Radio ad of 30 seconds duration

Magazine or newspaper ad

Bumper sticker

Brief skit

Paraphrase

DEVELOP/GENERALIZATION

5-10 minutes
Any number of persons
Space to work in small groups

B3c

DEFINITIONS

To say the same thing in other words.

To restate in a way which makes the meaning more obvious.

The stating of a text in parallel language, i.e., in words more modern and/or simple and/or interpretive.

DESIGN

The basic documents of the Christian religion are dated in the sense that they were written far in the past and, often, in another language. Those documents include the Bible, the creeds, confessional statements, and the catechisms. They can be paraphrased in order to make their meaning clearer.

The ability to restate something in our own words without changing the meaning shows that the broad educational goal of *comprehension* has been accomplished.

Research supports the belief that we remember better what we put in our own words. *Remembering* is a second broad educational goal that the paraphrase achieves.

DIRECTIONS

1. Be sure that the paraphrase is an appropriate method and that there is time for it in the lesson. It is appropriate if you can answer "yes" for the class to one or more of these questions:

Will the paraphrase increase their understanding?

Will the paraphrase enable them to remember it better?

Can the paraphrase enhance the meaning of the statement?

Can the paraphrase assist in sharing the meaning of the statement?

2. Decide precisely what you will have paraphrased. You may wish to restrict it to a key verse or sentence, a paragraph, a question and answer of the catechism, etc. Generally speaking, the smallest amount of material which fully includes the principle is desirable.

3. Select a method of grouping for the paraphrasing work. It may be done by individuals, pairs, small groups, or the whole class.

4. Determine how the groups who prepare the paraphrases will present them to the class (by reading, putting up in written form, etc.).

5. Decide if and how the class will respond to the paraphrases. Some options for responding are presented in Exercise 3.

B3c Paraphrase

1. EXAMPLE:
Three Published Paraphrases

When I'm beat, I need you, Lord,
So I hope you hear me
If you keep the score who could beat you?
But we don't think you will forget to
Hear us ask you for help.

So we just wait for you
To make us feel better inside.

(Psalm 130)[1]

But, in whatever way another acts big, I'll act big too. (Remember, I'm just kidding.) They are *Americans*—like me. They are *Anglo-Saxons*—like me . . . They are Christians—I'm talking like I'm nuts—I have it all over them. Here's my score:

Days on the work gang—lost count
Number times in jail—lost count
Number times beaten up—too many
Faced with death—quite often
The usual mauling by the State Patrol—five times
Shot—once
Car wrecks—three
Day and night in the swamp—once.

(2 Corinthians 11:21b–27)[2]

During childhood I talked, thought, and reasoned in concrete language and ideas; since becoming an adult I have spoken, thought, and used logic abstractly.

(1 Corinthians 13:11)[3]

2. EXERCISE:
Your Reactions to Example 1*

a. Which do you like best? Why?

b. What groups might find one or more of these paraphrases (1) comforting or helpful, (2) threatening, and (3) more understandable? State the reasoning behind your opinions.

c. What are the strengths and weaknesses of paraphrasing the scripture to "apply it to my group right now"?

3. EXERCISE:
Responding to Paraphrases

After reading each paraphrase in Example 1, give it the statement number(s) which applies:

1. Most meaningful to me
2. Most creative statement
3. Most faithful to the biblical text
4. Most memorable
5. Most free of jargon: easiest to understand

If this exercise is done in a group, members may share their views with each other. If you find that any of the statements above do not apply to at least one of the paraphrases, write a paraphrase to which it would apply.

NOTE: This exercise may be used with the *slogan*, also.

4. EXERCISE:
Suggestions for Paraphrase

a. The Lord's Prayer
b. Selected (by you) catechism questions and answers
c. The Apostles' Creed
d. The Nicene Creed

---

[1]Reprinted from *Treat Me Cool, Lord* by Carl F. Burke, © 1968. By permission of New Century Publishers, Inc., Piscataway, N.J.

[2]Reprinted from *The Cotton Patch Version of Paul's Epistles*, by Clarence Jordan, © 1968. By permission of New Century Publishers, Inc., Piscataway, N.J.

[3]Author's paraphrase.

*You may wish to know, in answering these questions, that the first paraphrase was written by a chaplain for tough street kids who were in jail. The second was penned by the founder of the Koinonia Farm in Americus, Georgia, which, like its founder, survived the civil rights struggle of the 1960s.

conclude
with precision and power

People react to all experiences, including educational ones, in some combination of these ways: thinking, feeling, and doing. These three human reactions are paralleled and focused by the three methods categories used to conclude lessons: Summarization, Celebration, and Application.

Where a significant amount of information has been thought through, Summarization methods (C2) are most appropriate. This category, placed in the center of the chart because it is used most often, includes *fill-in-the-blank test* (C2a) and *content chart presentation* (C2b).

To the left of Summarization is Application (C1). Its presence on the chart recognizes the besetting sin of so many classes, to spend 99% of the time on the information and 1% on *doing* something about it. Too often teachers waste even the 1% by concluding with vagueness (". . . and the point of this lesson is that we should all work at loving Jesus more") or with the lonely solution (". . . and only in our heart of hearts can each one of us find what this lesson tells us we ought to do . . .") This category gives us two ways to react: by *setting goals* (C1a) and *taking a position* (C1b).

The other category, Celebration (C3), is what most of us call "feeling." It includes such important acts as affirming (as in saying the creed with meaning), appreciating (as in sharing our emotional reaction to a Christian promise or truth), supporting (as in praying for a discovered need), and many other more-than-rational human reactions. Well known liturgical forms, the *litany* (C3a) and the *cinquain* (C3b), make up this category.

Jesus told us to love God with all of our heart, soul, strength, and mind (Luke 10:27), indicating his belief in feeling, doing, and thinking. Thus, the teacher who asks, "Which is the best category of method with which to conclude this lesson?" is one who follows Jesus' example of teaching the *whole* student.

When you place these **TEACH**NIQUES pages in a notebook, write on them your revision of steps, time estimates, strengths/weakness, or any other information. As you discover other methods that you like to use, create your own pages. Your notebook of teachniques should contain concise information on all the methods that you are using and trying to master.

begin

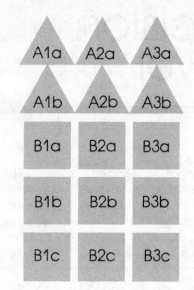

develop

B1a	B2a	B3a
B1b	B2b	B3b
B1c	B2c	B3c

HOW TO
conclude with precision and power

If the content should be used immediately use	If a large body of information has been studied use	If there is something to affirm or strengthen use
APPLICATION METHODS	**SUMMARIZATION METHODS**	**CELEBRATION METHODS**
C1a Goal Setting	C2a Fill in the Blank	C3a Litany
C1b Position Statement	C2b Content Chart Presentation	C3b Cinquain

Goal Setting

CONCLUDE/APPLICATION

5-10 minutes
Any number of persons
Space for small groups

DEFINITIONS

A statement of exactly what a person or group will do within a specific time-frame.

A statement of minimal accomplishments projected by and for a person or group as an expression of Christian responsibility.

DESIGN

Goal setting encourages Christians to link scripture to life.

Goal setting can move Christian students from a vague sense of general responsibility to a conviction of specific accountability.

Goal setting is a prerequisite to intelligent commitment. It's how one says, "I'll do this by then."

Goal setting can motivate Christian behavior. When people set and achieve specific goals, their satisfaction encourages them to set more goals. The alternative is for people to have a vague feeling that they ought to be doing far more than they can possibly imagine and, therefore, to ignore specific responsibilities that seem so minute. Goal achievement can lead to pride, but goal ignoring is sloth. Both are "deadly" sins.

DIRECTIONS

1. Decide or let the group decide whether individual or group goals will be set. If group goals are set, then break the larger group into smaller ones for that work.

2. Teach or rehearse the criteria for a goal.

   G = Grade: Can you be "graded" in terms of 100% or a lesser amount of achievement?

   O = Opportunity: Can you do this *where* you live *as* you are?

   A = Act: Is it an observable deed that you do?

   L = Limit: Have you set a date by which, or a time frame in which, the deed must be done?

3. After goals are written, it is helpful to have people critique each other's goals to be sure they meet the above criteria. The ultimate frustration is to set a goal which you can't achieve because you wrote it improperly. Group goals should be posted as a reminder as the time elapses.

Commentary on the Directions

1. We are touching on dangerous and sensitive ground when we structure goal setting. It may be wise, therefore, to get group approval for "public" goal setting and also provide for those who wish to do this in private.

2. There are many valid goals that this method won't touch directly. Most of these have to do with qualities hard to measure directly: more *love* for Christ, a greater *willingness* to serve, *thoughts* on a higher plane, a higher *care* factor, etc. These are worthy in and of themselves, but we can only measure what we will be *doing* when we have more of those qualities, not the qualities themselves.

3. When you set the date by which goals are to be accomplished, mark your teaching calendar to alert you to have the group check itself. To "set and forget" goals is a contradiction in terms.

C1a Goal Setting

1. EXAMPLE

Fran studied the criteria for goal setting and wrote four goals (left column). Then, in checking back over the criteria, she found and noted one error in each goal (middle column). Finally, Fran rewrote each goal to make it completely correct (right column).

GOALS WRITTEN AFTER THE FIRST STUDY	ERROR NOTED IN GOAL	CORRECTED GOAL STATEMENT
I will improve my memorization of the catechism questions we study for next Sunday's class.	Grade (percent achieved)	By Sunday I will be able to recite the answers to at least 8 of the 10 catechism questions we're studying.
I will share the story of my commitment to the Christian faith with youth by the end of Lent.	Opportunity (you can do it)	I'll share the story of my Christian commitment with the youth group by Easter if I'm recruited as advisor.
I'll try to do a better job of teaching this quarter.	Act (an observable deed)	I'll use at least one new method in my class each month in this quarter.
We're going to start tithing our take-home paychecks.	Limit (date set to be done)	We will tithe our take-home paychecks for this calendar year.

2. EXERCISE

Each of the goals below has one major fault. Indicate that fault using the letters G, O, A, or L (see middle column above) and correct it as has been done in 1 and 5. (see answers upside down below.)

__G__ 1. I'm going to cut back on my smoking next week. I don't believe in it. (I'll cut my smoking by 50% next week.)

_____ 2. By next Sunday I'll attempt to restore a broken relationship with an old friend.

_____ 3. A fellow church member who owes me money refuses to pay. I'll have the pastor and church officers talk to us before going to court.

_____ 4. I plan to give the next year of my retirement to God to make up for the mess I made of my life for the first 66 years.

__A__ 5. We pledge to not go to bed angry with our spouses or our children this week. (If we feel angry with spouse or child, we pledge to ask for forgiveness by the end of every day of this week.)

_____ 6. We will stop bragging to our friends that our preacher is better than theirs.

_____ 7. We will comfort our widowed parents whom we can only visit in the summer by calling them on a regular basis.

_____ 8. We'll attempt to spend at least 15 minutes daily with the Lord until New Year's Day, when we'll reevaluate our goals.

3. EXERCISE

Each of the goals in Exercise 2 was based on one of the following scripture passages. Place the number of the goal in the blank preceding each passage. (See answers upside down below.)

a. _____ Matthew 5:21-26

b. _____ Matthew 18:15-20

c. _____ 1 Corinthians 3:1-9

d. _____ 1 Corinthians 3:16-17

e. _____ 2 Corinthians 1:3-7

f. _____ Ephesians 4:25-26

g. _____ Philippians 3:13

h. _____ Revelation 3:15-16

Position Statement

CONCLUDE/APPLICATION

5-15 minutes
Any number of persons
Space for small groups

DEFINITIONS

A reasoned reaction to a pressing religious problem created to enlighten the writers and readers.

A paragraph containing:

(a) a concise statement of the problem

(b) set in its context,

(c) with a directed religious response to it, and

(d) undergirded by scriptural and theological reasons.

DESIGN

Position statements are seen everywhere: government, business, education, law, nonprofit organizations, all make and take them.

Position statements are deeply rooted in the Judeo part of our Judeo-Christian tradition. The prophets, priests, sages, and rabbis either (1) took positions on issues they perceived and then taught the people or (2) responded to problems put to them by the people with teaching. Many of the councils of the church did the same thing.

Position statements are attempts, usually by a group today, to make up its collective mind as carefully as possible on a significant ethical issue. When a denomination does it the phrase, "the mind of the church," is often used.

DIRECTIONS

1. Much of the biblical material and virtually all of our current ethical studies state or imply some things we ought to do. If the study of the session lends itself to a relatively simple application which fits the position statement form, that method should be considered.

2. The first time this form is used it should be explained and illustrated. A summary of this definition and an illustration should be left posted for mind refreshing when it will be used again or when new group members ask for a brief introduction to it. One way to introduce a position statement is given at the top of the following page.

3. This is a group method: decide the size and number of groups you will have and how they will be constituted (e.g., the leader appoints, they get together where they are, they select their groups, number off, etc.).

4. Give the groups the issue on which they are to take a position and appropriate biblical and theological books and resources.

5. Instruct each group on

(a) how long it has to work,

(b) how it should function (i.e., should it appoint a leader and/or reporter?), and

(c) the form its report should take (oral, written, poster, etc.).

6. Determine how the position statements will be presented and used. Decide if you wish to store the reports for future use in the unit or in other sessions.

1. EXAMPLE: An Introduction to the Method

Teacher:	"To conclude our study today I'll ask small groups to prepare position statements. You have in hand a simple, one-paragraph illustration of a position statement which is based on the issue described in 1 Corinthians 11:17–22, 27–34. On the board I have listed four factors in this crisis found in the printed statements. Help me identify those factors as we read through this position statement."

	Problem Stated	*Context Given* (What caused it)	*Church's Position* (Instruction)	*Reasoning Behind* (Theology)
Printed on the board:	"Profaning" the body and blood of Christ.	Drunk members at the Lord's Supper and no food left for late-comers.	Eat and drink for nourishment at home. No more "church suppers."	The supper is to anticipate the *heavenly* feast, but the way it is being celebrated reflects the opposite.

Printed handouts:	When the problem of discord at the love feast/Lord's Supper of First Church, Corinth was reported to Paul, he called it "profaning the body and blood of Christ." Pagan converts, apparently, were carrying into the church their old practice of overeating and getting drunk. The late-arriving members, who were much poorer (some would be slaves), were humiliated because little food was left for them. Paul ordered them all to eat their meals at home, but the Lord's Supper in "church." The Supper was to anticipate the harmony, equality, and blessing of the heavenly feast, not the gluttony, callousness, and indiscretion of the pagan past.
	Definition: A position statement is a reasoned reaction to a pressing religious problem created to enlighten the writers and readers.

2. EXERCISE: Current Church Position Statement

Virtually every church (i. e., denomination) has taken and continues to take positions on important issues, such as abortion, world peace, capital punishment, the population crisis, pornography, etc. These are published with supporting biblical and theological information and reasons in the church's official documents. Often a summary of all current positions is available in booklet form. This booklet is most useful for finding what the mind of the church is and for ascertaining where the original, complete position statement can be found. Inquire about the availability of such a booklet from your denomination.

3. EXERCISE: Your Current Curriculum Literature

Look over lessons or topics for the group that you will teach. Find a topic with an issue that the church has taken a position on, indicate its four factors (see Example 1), and write a position statement which includes all four of those factors.

Fill in the Blank

CONCLUDE/SUMMARIZATION

3-6 minutes
Any number of persons
No space requirements

C2a

DEFINITIONS

A test form made up of statements in which the missing word or phrase expresses the concept the student is to remember. It may also take the form of a series of questions which take specific words or phrases as answers.

DESIGN

Fill in the blank is a nearly "objective" test form, meaning that there is, ideally, just one correct answer. The answers can be corrected with a key by a person ignorant of the subject. Perfectly objective types (true-false, multiple choice, matching) can be corrected by a machine.

Fill in the blank is a natural form of test for both student and teacher because it is most like the oral questioning process. Teachers are more likely to try it before attempting to write other types of "objective" tests.

Many people dislike completely subjective or objective tests. The former, usually essay, take too much time to write and grade. The latter appear only to measure *recognition* of the right answer. Fill in the blank is easily written and graded, and measures *recall* of important concepts.

DIRECTIONS

1. The concepts to be tested should be important information indicated in the lesson objectives. Don't test for trivia!

2. When this kind of test is used informally to help the student check his or her learning, it does *not* matter where the blanks are in the sentence. Only when many tests have to be checked by one teacher is the format (placing the blanks uniformly so they can be checked quickly by a key) a matter of concern.

3. Be sure a single answer is called for by the statement or question. You may structure the answer by indicating the class or type of answer you want. For instance, *"How many people* did Jesus say knew when he would return?" is better than "Who knew when he would return, according to Jesus?" In the second question all these answers would be correct: "No one," "Only God," "Nobody."

4. Limit the number of blanks to be filled in to one or two in each statement.

5. Make the language used in the item so simple that the least verbal person in your group will not have trouble understanding what you want.

6. Don't give the answer to one item away in another item.

7. You may wish to give the students some standard of judgment to reward good performance while not embarrassing those who didn't do well. Have them correct their own tests according to humorous criteria:

0 to 3 correct: Try getting to bed on Saturday night.

4 to 6 correct: You must have paid attention this morning—thank you!

7 to 9 correct: Obviously you did your homework and were on your toes today—blessed art thou!

10 correct: Congratulations! The good news is that you may exempt taking this class. The bad news is that you've been made part of the teaching team.

C2a Fill in the Blank

1. EXAMPLE: A Test on the Transition from Joshua (the Conquest) to the Judges

1. The Philistines controlled the coastal plain with ease because of a weapon they had which was perfect for that purpose. That weapon, which devastated infantry, was the _____ . (Judges 1:19)

2. The Jews lacked the weapon named in the above item and good weapons for their infantry because they were still in the _____ age. (Exodus 38:2-11)

3. The Jewish farmers were dependent upon the Philistines who could _____ their agricultural tools for a fee. (1 Samuel 13:10-23)

4. In Joshua's closing address to Israel he asserted that if they were faithful to God, God would _____ them from their enemies; but if they accepted "other" gods, their enemies would _____ them. (Joshua 23:1-13)

5. This cause-effect relationship in the preceding item is called by one scholar the "Deuteronomic formula for _____ ." (Joshua 1:7-8)

6. Later, a whole book of the Bible will be written in which a man wrestles with why this formula doesn't work for him. The name of the man and book is _____ .

---

2. EXERCISE: Identifying Flaws in Fill-in-the-Blank Items

Match the flaws from the list (using the letters A, B, C, G, & L) with the items they describe and explain your reasons in writing. The first one has been done as an illustration for you. Answers are upside down below.

__C__ 1. The first judge to be mentioned in the book of Judges is __Othniel__ . (The knowledge that Othniel is *first* is not important. Judges 3:9)

_____ 2. The fact that the Israelites were virtually forced to give up their amphictyony (tribal confederacy) to accept a monarch at the end of the Judges is a sign of their great _____ .

_____ 3. The nation system in which the tribes gathered only for war and worship was called an _____ .

_____ 4. The principal _____ of Israel during the period of the _____ was the religion of the _____ , _____ .

_____ 5. Though the term "Judge" is conceptualized contemporarily as one who adjudicates, and though these biblical personages in several cases performed that worthy function, it is clear from our study of the Bible that the common behavior of all the Judges was _____ .

Flaws

Answers: Specific enough?

Blanks: Two or less?

Concept: Worth remembering?

Give away: Answer found in another item?

Language: Simple enough?

Exercise 2:

2. The answer is "strength"; the flaw is A because many other nouns could be true, such as "faith in Samuel."

3. The flaw is G: the answer, "amphictyony," is found in item #2.

4. Too many blanks (B) to lead to the answers: "temptation," "Judges," "Canaanites," and "Baalism."

5. L: answer is "Job."

54

Content Chart Presentation

CONCLUDE/SUMMARIZATION

2-5 minutes
Any number of persons
Space for all to see

C2b

DEFINITIONS

A listing of the main points of a session, printed large enough for all the group to read on a large sheet, the chart.

The brief verbal explanation of those points with the speaker focusing the group's attention on each point on the chart as it is explained: the presentation.

DESIGN

Content chart presentation combines the efficiency of the spoken paragraph with the visual "pegs" of summary to focus attention, reinforce the memory image, and enable the group to conclude with the "big picture" of what has been studied.

Content chart presentation tends to "force" the leader who prepares it to have a well-organized session, because it often provides painful visual feedback for illogical, inconsistent, or vague points.

In a long, complex unit (often historical) a series of content charts can picture the sequence of a series of events and their meaning.

Since a content chart is a stored memory device for the group, it can be a review device for the next session.

DIRECTIONS

1. Write an outline of the points made in the session.

2. *If* you are in a unit in which you wish to use a series of charts as a visual record of what you've studied, look at the rest of the sessions to see if there is some way to link all the charts together. "Linkage" means putting common information in the same position on each chart so that when the charts are placed side by side, the eye can follow the sequence from left to right. Illustrations of "common information" would be dates, key persons, doctrinal issues, events, applications, etc.

3. Make your content chart with letters large enough for all the group to read. It may be made on poster board, a large sheet of newsprint, etc. The clever use of color will improve your production.

4. Write the summary paragraph of what you will say, getting it into interesting, logical, and memorable form. This exercise will enable you to speak without depending on your notes (students *hate* to be read to) and to give your attention to the chart, calling attention to points as you make them and having good eye contact with the group the remainder of the time.

5. Decide if you wish to cover your points with pieces of paper taped over each. As you introduce each point you would remove its cover and reveal it to the class. This procedure will encourage the class to concentrate on the point on which you're talking and not to read ahead.

C2b Content Chart Presentation

1. EXAMPLE: A Linking Chart for a Unit on the Parables

NAME OF PARABLE	The Sower, The Four Soils	The Two Sons
FOUND WHERE?	Matthew 13:1–23 Mark 4:1–20 Luke 8:4–15	Matthew 21:28–32
TOLD TO WHOM?	The people by the sea	
PARTICIPANTS	Sower, seed, 4 soils.	A father, his two sons.
STORY SYNOPSIS	Sower's seeds fell on the path, rocky and good soil, but grew only on the last.	When asked to work in the vineyard, the first son refused but went, the second politely agreed, but didn't.
MEANING	The word dies in evil, shallow, or pleasure-loving people. The receptive share it with many.	Polite talk is no substitute for responsible Christian behavior.
OUR RESPONSE	What kind of person am I? Am I bearing fruit?	Do I produce what I promise?

2. EXERCISE:
Critique a Content Chart on Magic

(a) Is there too much? If so, what should go?

(b) Would it be better to have one illustration for each "type" named (e.g., Saul and the Witch of Endor) instead of listing all the Bible passages?

(c) How could this poster be changed in form to communicate better?

(d) How could color improve this poster?

(e) What do you think the spoken paragraph accompanying it would be?

3. EXERCISE:
Critique Your Own Content Chart

Create a content chart using material that you will be teaching. Write the summary paragraph and present your chart to fellow beginning teachers. Ask them to critique it using the criteria in Exercise 2 above and under DIRECTIONS on the previous page.

MAGIC: THREAT TO THE RELIGION OF YAHWEH

Magic: Use of superhuman powers to control and foreknow.

TYPES	FUNCTION	BIBLICAL ILLUSTRATIONS
Diviner	Predicter	Acts 16:16 ff.; Ezekiel 21:21; Genesis 44:5
Augurer	Predicter	Isaiah 47:13; 1 Samuel 28:8ff
Soothsayer	Dream interpreter	Daniel 4:7, 9; 5:11, 12; 2:27; Acts 16:16
Charmer, Sorcerer, or Witch	Spell caster	Exodus 7:11; Acts 8:9–24; 13:6–12
Medium, Wizard, or Necromancer	Consults with spirits of the dead	1 Samuel 28:8 ff.
Priest and worshiper	Participate in fertility cycle	Deuteronomy 23:17–18

People always want to control their fate. Whatever promises this power is very attractive. God says, "Trust me. I control nature."

Litany

CONCLUDE/CELEBRATION

1-3 minutes to do/5-12 minutes to create
Any number of leaders and participants
No space requirements

C3a

DEFINITIONS

A litany is a prayer prayed responsively by leader and people.

A litany is a prayer, typically of intercession, petition, praise, etc., in which the leader speaks a series of statements which develop a theme, and the people answer each statement with (typically) a common response.

DESIGN

A litany focuses the attention of the group better than a leader-prayed prayer of similar length by subdividing the prayer into a series of short, specific points prayed by the leader, interspersed with a refrain prayed by the people.

A litany involves the leader and people actively in the prayer because both pray aloud. Though the leader's part appears to be more important because it is a series *(What* we pray for and *why)*, the people's unchanging response is stronger in language because it addresses God and tells what is requested.

Beginners tend to perceive a litany as much easier than writing a "long prayer" because the litany arrangement enables them to "divide and conquer."

DIRECTIONS

1. Choose the *theme* of the prayer and put it in the title.

2. Identify the *type* of prayer. You may wish to put this identifying word in the title (e.g., "A Litany of *Intercession* for Medical Missionaries").* The type will determine the form of response (e.g., "Lord, hear our intercession on behalf of these ministers of healing").

3. Write the series of leader's statements.

4. *How* you do numbers 1-3 above can vary in many ways. For instance:

   (a) The whole group could do 1 and 2 by discussion and, after agreeing which small groups will create the intercessions and for which healers (the hospital, physicians, nurses, laboratory technicians, aides, etc.), each small group could work separately.

   (b) The whole prayer could be created by the whole group through discussion.

   (c) Each small group could create and present in written form on newsprint a series of statements specified in number 3 above. The group would choose the most meaningful of these to pray in their litany.

5. How litanies are prayed can be varied also. Different groups may wish to be the "leader" for their statements.

*Some other types are Praise, Thanksgiving, Confession, Petition.

1. EXAMPLE: First Portion of a Litany on Psalm 107

People: O give thanks to the Lord, for he is good; he has delivered and redeemed us, his people.

Leader: Some of us nearly died in the desert, unable to find the city of God until he led to the straight and narrow way.

People: O give thanks to the Lord, for he is good; he has delivered and redeemed us, his people.

Leader: Some of us were in the darkness of prison, chained to . . .

2. EXERCISE: Litany of Intercession for Medical Missionaries

In the DIRECTIONS given on the previous page, a type, title, and ideas for a series of leader statements were given. Develop this into a litany. If you are working in a group of teachers doing this activity, compare your litanies to see how many different ways just this one prayer could be written.

3. EXERCISE

Here is a blessing which can be sung as a round:

"For health and strength and daily food we praise thy name, O Lord."*

Put this song into litany form, explaining each step of the process. Include the title, type, and parts for people and leader.

4. EXERCISE: Cataloging Psalms

Many portions of Psalms, the hymnbook of the Hebrews, can be put into litany form easily. Since psalms cover many topics, it would be good exercise to catalog them by type and give each a name. Thus, when your lesson calls for worship centered around a particular topic, you can use a psalm related to that topic. I have listed ten psalms. You are to catalog eight of them. I've done two.

Psalm	Type	Suggested Name for Litany
8	Praise/Adoration	The Majesty of the Creator's Name
23		
29		
67		
88		
90		
91		
103		
107:1-32	Thanksgiving	Our Deliverer and Redeemer

*The song "For Health and Strength" is used with permission of G. Schirmer, Inc.

Cinquain
CONCLUDE/CELEBRATION

5-10 minutes
Any number of persons
No space requirements

DEFINITIONS

A French five (cinq) line poetry form having (in that order) one-, two-, three-, four-, and one-word lines.

Typical content of the five lines:

1. A one-word title
2. A two-word description
3. A three-word action phrase or word grouping
4. A four-word emotion phrase or word grouping; and
5. One word referring to the title in a creative way.

DESIGN

A cinquain is such a short and simple nonrhyming form that even those who lack self-confidence in poetry are generally willing to try it. Therefore, in the area of poetic expression, the cinquain is an ideal form to try first.

The cinquain provides an opportunity for creativity within the comfort of a structure. It can be thought of as a "fill-in-the-blanks" type of poetry for those who require the security of structure. For those who thrive on freedom it can be presented as an opportunity for infinite variety within a simple form.

DIRECTIONS

1. If the group is not familiar with the cinquain, you will need to explain the form and give one illustration of it. To do this, give out the following form to each person and present your illustration (which could be Example 1 on the other side of this page) to show them how it's done.

CINQUAIN

My statement of truth to be celebrated:

Title of poem   _____

Description of title   _____ _____

Action words/phrase   _____ _____ _____

Emotion words/phrase   _____ _____ _____ _____

Another word about the
   title or theme of the poem   _____

2. Decide if each individual will write a cinquain or if they will be created in small groups. If groups, decide how the groups will be formed.

3. Each person or group should write out in a clear statement the truth that their cinquain will attempt to express. Precision of thought is a precondition of penetrating poetry.

4. Assign a length of time and inform the group as to how they will share their creations.

5. As the poets work, monitor them so that you can lengthen or shorten the time as needed.

I am indebted to Donald L. Griggs' workshop for introducing me to this method. See also *The Princeton Encyclopedia of Poetry and Poetics,* Alex Preminger, ed. (Princeton University Press, 1965), p. 126; *The Oxford Companion to American Literature,* James D. Hart (New York: Oxford University Press, 1956); and the *Histoire du vers francais,* vol. II (1951).

C3b Cinquain

1. EXAMPLES: Two Teachers on Teaching

Teaching

Demanding   Rewarding

Study   Plan   Pray

Fascinating Frustrating Fatiguing Fantastic

Service

Teaching

Significant service

A team effort

Our calling from God

Hallelujah!

2. EXERCISE

Create a cinquain which celebrates your calling as a Christian teacher.

_____

_____ _____

_____ _____ _____

_____ _____ _____ _____

_____

3. EXAMPLES

These are cinquains written from the viewpoints of the Jew and the Samaritan after . . . (Luke 10: 30–37).

Neighbor:

Samaritan.   Gentile.

Traveling.   Dying Jew.

But he's a person!

Hurry!

Neighbor:

A Jew.

Traveling.   Robbed.   Beaten.

Help, priest, Levite!   Oh!!

Neighbor.

4. EXERCISE

Take curriculum material which has a point to be celebrated and write one or two cinquains. If you don't have curriculum handy, write the after-reflection of the prodigal son and his older brother instead.

_____

_____ _____

_____ _____ _____

_____ _____ _____ _____

_____

see
the big picture

I'm sure that you've purchased many things which said, "Can be assembled by an average kindergartener," or "A simple half-hour project." Then, you had to call in a mechanical engineer, lathe operator, and therapist before you got it together and recovered your composure. What looks so easy on paper often is difficult in practice.

In the past three chapters you've been taught a system of methods selection and lesson planning which appears simple. Now it's time to show you how that system looks in real life so that you can be the judge of how easy it is.

Three example lessons are presented in the pages which follow. The format of each is the same. In the left-hand column the planning process is recorded (plans one and three) or the lesson is given in detail (plan two). The right-hand column shows you how the methods taught in this book are used in these lesson plans. In fact, some of the examples given on the teachniques pages appear here in the context of a complete lesson.

Each lesson planning example concludes with a lesson plan and chart highlighting the actual methods used in that lesson. This page should be removed before you read an example. The first time you read the example put the lesson plan next to the pages as you read them. You will see how the lesson plan actually used emphasizes procedures, not content. What is done by whom for how many minutes using which forms/materials—not each word spoken by the teacher(s)—makes the plan. Read the example a second time and follow the flow of the methods on the diagram at the bottom of the page which you have removed. That flow is like the skeleton which supports the flesh and muscle of the body of the lesson. It is not visible, but it holds the lesson together.

Each example in this chapter is a radically different type of lesson. The first is a formal church school class for youth ages 12–14 who are studying the life and work of Moses. In it an experienced and an apprentice teacher share in the planning process. The second is the plan used by one adult teacher in an informal setting with older youth, ages 15–18. It also focuses on a portion of scripture. The third example is the final planning of a lesson for an adult class on a controversial and complicated subject, the relationship of church and state. In these three examples two-thirds of the methods and all of the nine categories on the flow chart are used.

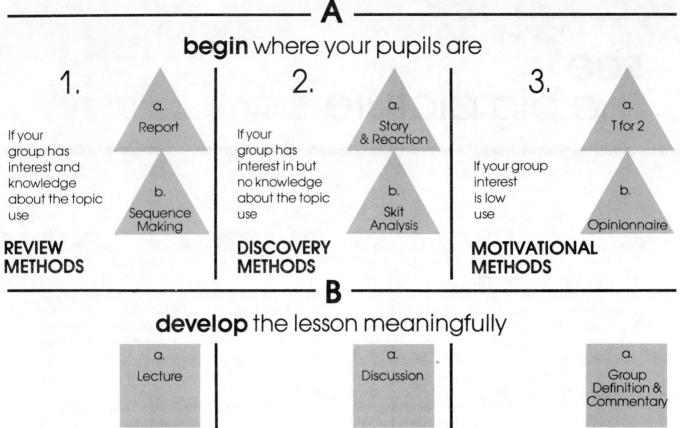

A

begin where your pupils are

1.

If your group has interest and knowledge about the topic use

a. Report

b. Sequence Making

REVIEW METHODS

2.

If your group has interest in but no knowledge about the topic use

a. Story & Reaction

b. Skit Analysis

DISCOVERY METHODS

3.

If your group interest is low use

a. T for 2

b. Opinionnaire

MOTIVATIONAL METHODS

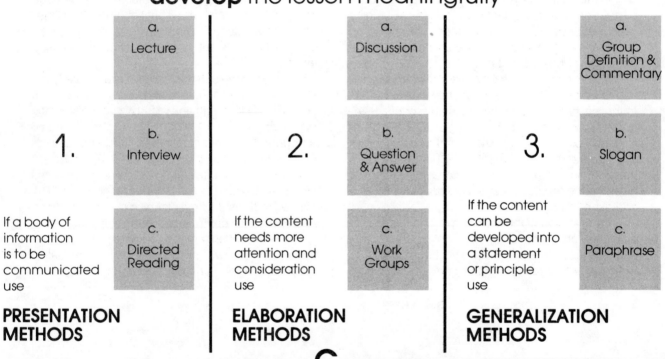

B

develop the lesson meaningfully

1.

If a body of information is to be communicated use

a. Lecture

b. Interview

c. Directed Reading

PRESENTATION METHODS

2.

If the content needs more attention and consideration use

a. Discussion

b. Question & Answer

c. Work Groups

ELABORATION METHODS

3.

If the content can be developed into a statement or principle use

a. Group Definition & Commentary

b. Slogan

c. Paraphrase

GENERALIZATION METHODS

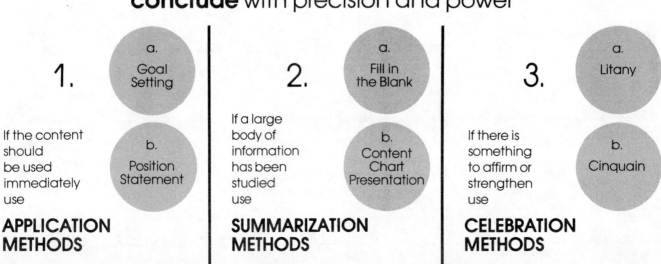

C

conclude with precision and power

1.

If the content should be used immediately use

a. Goal Setting

b. Position Statement

APPLICATION METHODS

2.

If a large body of information has been studied use

a. Fill in the Blank

b. Content Chart Presentation

SUMMARIZATION METHODS

3.

If there is something to affirm or strengthen use

a. Litany

b. Cinquain

CELEBRATION METHODS

Lesson Planning Example One

Pat and Lynn's Planning Session

Teachers: Pat, an experienced lead teacher
Lynn, a new assistant teacher

Group: A class of bright, motivated youth, ages 12-14

Time: 60-70 minutes

Lesson Title: *Moses Makes His Move*

Scripture: Exodus 2:23—3:22

Materials: Curriculum books, Bibles, map, newsprint, marker, and duplicated sheets

Seating: Three tables with six chairs each

Pat: Well, this week we'll study Exodus 2:23—3:22, 25 verses. Let me see, you were to prepare a brief review activity and it's my turn to set the scene or prepare the class in some way. What have you got?

Lynn: It's been just two weeks since we've finished our unit on the Patriarchs. As they arrive, those who haven't read the scripture beforehand will read the passage while the rest work on this big "E" shaped form *(method A1b)*. I've given the approximate dates of the first Patriarch, Abraham, and this unit's hero, Moses, plus a few clues. Should this be done by individuals or table teams?

Pat: I prefer table teams, provided you assign who is to sit where in order to mix boys and girls, talkative and quiet, etc. This is a really clever activity. At this rate the class will be glad when I leave and you take over!

Lynn: I doubt if I can adequately replace you but I'm sure going to learn everything I can from you while you are in charge. Anyhow, working on this sequence will keep those active youngsters busy until everyone's arrived. How are you going to set the scene?

(continued on p. 64)

METHODS USED

Sequence Making (A1b)

The Hebrew People: The Big "E" Activity

In our study of Genesis 12 through Exodus 2 we have learned about these eight important personages:

Aaron   Esau   Jacob   Melchizedek
Abraham   Isaac   Joseph   Moses

Put them in historical order using the following chart. The three prongs of the "E" tell you that three pairs of these personages were contemporaries: therefore, they should be put side by side on the chart. Clues are provided. Consult the Bible to make and check your choices. It's a race. Go!

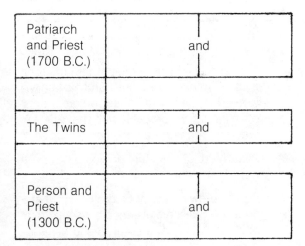

Patriarch and Priest (1700 B.C.)	and	
The Twins	and	
Person and Priest (1300 B.C.)	and	

Correctly made sequence:

Abraham and Melchizedek

Isaac

Jacob and Esau

Joseph

Moses and Aaron

Lesson Planning
Example One

Pat: Every week there are several class members who come early: their parents are teachers. I thought I'd ask them to prepare reports based on the study questions given in the pupil books *(method A1a)*. They can be prepared to answer all four of the questions, after consulting the map and pupil books for help. That will keep them productively busy and get everyone thinking about the meaning of the scripture.

Lynn: Sounds good. I'll assign one of the reporters to each of the three table teams. If any team completes its big "E" activity before the time is up, they can discuss one or more of the questions. That will give them more understanding of the scripture than if they just hear the reports.

Pat: Now, shouldn't we select our objectives? It seems to me that we can make either the struggle of Moses' decision or the meanings of the name of God our focus. We're not tied down to the objectives given in the curriculum, but they tend to be appropriate.

Lynn: Well, I think that how Moses thought of or defined God is more important than his decision. The class can understand but not fully appreciate how radical this decision must have been for Moses and his family. I would also like to emphasize some facts, even though we probably won't have time to test their recall for another lesson or so.

Pat: What facts of this story do you believe are most important?

Lynn: The Hebrew name for God: YHWH, what a "Hebrew" was, the distance between Egypt and Israel, the names Aaron and Miriam.

Pat: I'll support you 100%. Let's write our objectives now. The students will show that they have learned Moses' understanding of God this lesson. We'll test for their knowledge of those other facts later.

(continued on p. 65)

Report (A1a)

STUDY QUESTIONS

1. Assuming that Moses had heard of the king of Egypt's death, what might he have hoped for the condition of the Hebrew people under the new king? Why? (Exodus 2:23–25)

2. How does God identify himself to Moses? Why couldn't he have just said to Moses, "I'm God"? (3:6–14)

3. What did Moses do to show respect for God? Would you have done the same thing in that time and place? Why?

4. Why was it necessary for Moses to describe Canaan as a land "flowing with milk and honey"? (5:17) Measure the mileage from Egypt to Canaan on the map and think about what they would have had to go through. What might have happened if Moses had told the people about (a) the distance, (b) the desert, and (c) the strength of the Canaanites who lived there?

OBJECTIVES

1. The students (by table groups) will write Moses' definition of God, including God's special relationship to the Hebrews and his special assignment to Moses.

2. The students will be able to define or identify *YHWH, Moses, Aaron, Miriam,* and *Hebrew* by the end of this unit.

Lesson Planning
Example One

Lynn: I'm comfortable with that.

Pat: Let me see where we are in the lesson plan. About ten minutes into the class hour you have the tables present their "E" for Exodus review, correcting any mistakes that are made. Why don't you also have the opening prayer and call for the reports on the scripture study. Make sure that everyone has a Bible open to the passage so that when verses are pointed out they can follow along. I don't think that we should discuss those questions too much because we could get into the information found in the Moses interview *(method B1b)* suggested in the teacher's manual—unless you don't think that we should use that interview?

Lynn: On the contrary, I think that the interview idea is just great. I feel that there are more questions than we'll have time to cover, but it's always comforting to have more questions than you need . . . just in case you misjudged the time.

Pat: I get the feeling that you'd prefer to do the interviewing rather than be interviewed.

Lynn: How right you are! And I think that you and I ought to do the interview for two reasons. First, I don't think anyone but you knows enough about the story to answer these questions. Second, we've just had them do two activities, actually three if they read the Bible passage. They'll be ready for us to present something to them.

Pat: I'll concede. How do you want to do the interview?

Lynn: Let's pretend that it's a TV talk show and that you're the guest because you're a prominent local person with a rather dramatic (or should I say, "weird"?) idea.

Pat: Sounds good to me. Let's put it down.

(continued on p. 66)

Interview (B1b)

Interviewer:

This is Iszekiah of SBC (Sinai Broadcasting Company). Today we have a man with us who believes that his work is to compel Egypt to release its Hebrew slaves and make them into a nation which can conquer Canaan! Please give a cordial welcome to Moses, a man with a big dream!

> I can tell by your accent that you're not a Sinai native. Tell us about yourself, especially about your escape from death in infancy.
>
>> Who are the Hebrews and why are they special?
>>
>> Couldn't you just be having a mid-life crisis? Didn't your foster parents treat you well?
>>
>> Show us an image of your God. What is his specialty—war, fertility, good personal fortune? Where does he act—in the hills, deserts, etc.? Who is his consort?

Egypt is "the" power in this area. How do you propose to get them to free your fellow Hebrews without a tremendous army? Do you have a plan?

> How do you know these Hebrews really want to be free?
>
> How will you get them organized?
>
> Here is a map. What route do you plan to take and how can you avoid the Egyptian military camps along the coastal highway?

Moses, this is an overwhelming task. Why not just stay here in Sinai and enjoy the good life with your family?

> 1. How does your family feel about this plan?
> 2. Is anybody going to help you?

Tie Up: What do you anticipate as your greatest challenges in freeing these slaves and making a nation out of them?

Lesson Planning
Example One

Pat: We've probably used up two-thirds of our time. How shall we accomplish our first objective? That will be the test of whether the class has been paying attention to the reports on the Bible passage and the Moses interview.

(A thoughtful silence)

I propose that we just have each table group prepare what they believe Moses' definition of God was at this time *(method B3a)*. It would help the class if we structured the definition—and save time, too.

Lynn: You mean, in terms of relationships?

Pat: Yes. Define God in terms of not only his name but to whom he related himself and what he wanted to happen to them.

Lynn: Oh, I see. That would make it easier.

Pat: In fact, it might increase the class's attention if you tell them, right after your prayer, that they ought to make mental notes of everything they hear that could be used in a definition of God, because we will be doing that later.

Lynn: I'd be glad to. Now, I assume that we'd better close.

Pat: Since time will be short I suggest a litany, one in which each table writes one statement *(method C3a)*. It would carry through the theme of God's choice of a nation to be obedient.

Lynn: That's fine with me if you'll do it and take charge of the closing.

Pat: Agreed.

Group Definition (B3a)

By table teams, write out what you believe Moses' definition of God was. Include in your definition God's name, to which people/nation God related himself, and what God wanted to accomplish through them. Take 5 to 7 minutes. Post it on newsprint.

Litany (C3a)

Table 1: Lord, you chose the Hebrews to be your special people. You gave the world the Messiah through them.

All: Thank you, God, for caring about the Hebrew people and the world.

Table 1: _____

All: Thank you, God, for caring about the Hebrew people and the world.

Table 2: Lord, you heard the cry of the enslaved Hebrews and used Moses to rescue them.

All: Thank you, God, for caring about the Hebrew people and the world.

Table 2: _____

All: Thank you, God, for caring about the Hebrew people and the world.

Table 3: Lord, you promised Moses that you would help him do the work of helping others.

All: Thank you, God, for caring about the Hebrew people and the world.

Table 3: _____

All: Thank you, God, for caring about the Hebrew people and the world. Through Jesus Christ our Lord. Amen.

Instructions: Each table is to create a statement for this litany carrying through the idea expressed in the statement given for that table: Table 1 should think of how God has blessed our country and can bless others through us. Table 2 could focus on our freedoms and the need for freedom throughout the world. Table 3 could affirm how God is with us today, seeking to work through us.

LESSON PLANNING EXAMPLE 1
The Lesson Plan Used by Pat and Lynn for Moses Makes His Move

Objectives: 1. The students (by table groups) will write Moses' definition of God, including God's special relationship to the Hebrews and his special assignment to Moses.

2. (for unit accomplishment) The students will be able to identify *YHWH, Moses, Aaron, Miriam,* and *Hebrew* by the end of the unit.

CLOCK TIME	METHODS	IN CHARGE	MATERIALS NEEDED
9:35	Give assignments to three early students.	Lynn	Curriculum (student) books, Bibles.
9:40	Ask others to read scripture if they havent. Give big "E" page assignment by tables.	Lynn	Placecards taped to table places Three "E's," one per table; Bibles
9:55	Hear and correct "E" sequence answers. Have opening prayer and share objective. Hear reports. Amplify as needed. (Be sure all Bibles open.)	Lynn	Big "E" on chalkboard
10:15	Introduce the interview. Do it. Open it up for audience questions till time's up.	Pat and Lynn	Interview questions (Lynn) ? Moses' costume? (Pat)
10:25	Do Moses' definition of God by tables.	Pat	Newsprint and marker at each table
10:35	Do litany. (If definitions come slowly, let slower workers continue with defining.) Post definitions for later use.	Pat	Duplicated copies of the litany form (have 18 on hand)
10:45	Use litany for closing worship.	Pat	

begin with REVIEW

A1a
Report

A1b
Sequence Making

develop by PRESENTATION and GENERALIZATION

B3a
Group Definition & Commentary

B1b
Interview

CONCLUDE with CELEBRATION

C3a
Litany

Lesson Planning Example Two

Noel Nelson's Youth Fellowship Program

Group: An informal group of older youth (ages 15–18), who are assumed to be motivated but not knowledgeable

Time: 40 minutes

Lesson Title: *A Tale of Two Temptations*

Scripture: James 2:1–9 and 1 Peter 5:6–10

Materials: Armbands, duplicated statements and work assignments, paper, pencils

Seating: In a circle or circles

Objective: The students will be able to state one temptation of a "persecuted" Christian and one of a "rewarded" Christian.

METHODS USED

Story and Reaction (A2a)

Teacher says (with a straight face):
"Today all the churches in our country were instructed to pass out these statements to the students of their membership. We have set this part of our time together to deal with this surprise development. Please read and discuss this statement very carefully and make your decisions about the armbands now.

Teacher hands out statements so that one student gets Statement A, the next one Statement B, etc., around the circle(s). All the statements look the same. While youth are reading the statements, an armband is placed in front of each.

Statement A

NOTICE TO ALL STUDENTS
FROM THE GOVERNMENT OFFICE
OF INTERNAL SECURITY:

The government, recognizing the great contribution of institutional Christianity, has ruled that Christian students, in high school or equivalent institutions, will be (1) given preference in seating on any form of public transportation, (2) receive a 5% discount on any purchase for which they pay cash, and (3) receive an annual stipend of $10 per year of age attained on Dec. 31 of each year that they are full-time students. To be eligible, youth must wear armbands at all times, except in their place of residence. You must make decision about wearing the armband before you leave this meeting.

Your leader may discuss this law with you as to its consequences, but not as to its rightness or wrongness. You should discuss it first and primarily with your peers. The armband is provided.

Statement B

NOTICE TO ALL STUDENTS
FROM THE GOVERNMENT OFFICE
OF INTERNAL SECURITY:

The government, fearful of the effect of various pressure groups, has ruled that all practicing Christians who are students in high school or similar institutions must wear identification armbands at all times, except when they are in their place of residence. Such persons will not be permitted to use credit cards, write checks, or obtain credit of any kind for purchases. If you plan to practice Christianity in any way (worship, youth meetings, etc.) you must wear this armband or be liable to imprisonment (1 year for the first offense). Before you leave this meeting you must make a decision about wearing the armband.

Your teacher or leader may discuss this law with you as to its consequences, but not as to its rightness or wrongness. You should discuss it first and primarily with your peers. The armband is provided.

Lesson Planning
Example Two

Teacher allows time for the youth to discuss this development with each other. (Say as little as possible, but press them for a decision to either put one on, or return it to you.) The youth will discover that every other person is either being offered a reward or being punished for being identified as a Christian.

Teacher extends the post-discovery reaction with discussion (method B2a).

Teacher breaks the youth into two work groups (method B2c). One will study the passage from James which deals with the temptation of privilege. The other will study a passage from 1 Peter in which Christians are being persecuted for being identified as Christians.

Teacher, sensing that both groups have finished their work, invites them to share their findings with each other. Teacher fills in the content chart (method C2b) as each group's conclusions are expressed and reacted to.

Teacher uses the content chart to give focus and closure to the issues raised in the session and then invites the students to conclude with the prayers they have prepared.

Discussion (B2a)

1. How did you feel about this decision? Why?

2. What were the issues which you considered—in relation to family, friends, future, etc.?

3. What would the church gain and lose if being religious were rewarded? if being religious were punished?

4. Which would be more difficult? Why?

Work Groups (B2c)

Group A studies James 2:1-9. Group B studies 1 Peter 5:6-10. Both groups will complete the same assignment:

1. What temptation did this group face?

2. Which Christians today face the same temptation?

3. Give this temptation a name.

4. Write a brief summary of its nature and how the scripture instructs Christians to respond to it.

5. Each group member should write a one-sentence prayer for some Christian group that faces this temptation today.

Content Chart Presentation (C2b)

TWO TEMPTATIONS

Name	Nature	We're to . . .
James 2:1-9 Snobbishness Condescension (in good times)	Denying others respect because they're less prosperous.	Treat all with respect. Beware of the temptations of wealth. Treat poor with special compassion.
1 Peter 5:6-10 Giving up in persecution Anxiety Depression	Prolonged, severe persecution leads to loss of hope.	Lean on God for strength. Keep on keeping on. Resist exhaustion as the devil's ploy. Expect God to strengthen us.

LESSON PLANNING EXAMPLE 2

The Lesson Plan Used by Noel Nelson for *A Tale of Two Temptations*

Objective: The students will be able to state one temptation of a persecuted Christian and one of a "rewarded" Christian.

CLOCK TIME	METHODS	MATERIALS NEEDED
7:10	Get everyone quiet. Ask them to remain quiet and study the sheets being given out. (Keep a grim face.) While they read, lay an armband in front of each person. (Sit back and let them begin and continue talking to each other!)	Statements from OFFICE OF INTERNAL SECURITY stacked so that A's and B's alternate Armbands
7:20	Lead the after-discovery discussion.	
7:30	Transition: point out that this is not a new problem. Have them do the Bible study by two work groups. (A's and B's)	Duplicated Bible study assignments (or put it on the chalkboard), Bibles, paper and pencils
7:40	Share the work assignments, which I put on the Content Chart as they're given.	Content chart on the chalkboard or newsprint
7:45	Amplify as needed . . . . . and close by going over the contrast.	
7:48	Sentence prayers of intercession for those facing two kinds of temptations conclude the session.	

begin with DISCOVERY

A2a
Story & Reaction

develop by ELABORATION

B2a
Discussion

B2c
Work Groups

conclude with SUMMARIZATION

C2b
Content Chart Presentation

Lesson Planning Example Three

3

Teaching Team Plans Adult Elective Class

Group: Issue-oriented adults of a wide age range

Time: 60 minutes

Unit Title: Issues in America

Lesson Title: *Church, State, and Public Schools*

Materials: Duplicated copies of the opinionnaire, newsprint report form for opinionnaire, skit scripts, paper and pencils

Seating: Rows of folding chairs facing the lectern, chalk and bulletin boards

Objectives: 1. The students will be able to define or illustrate "pluralism."

2. The students will be able to (a) identify and (b) take a position on two current issues in the Church, State, and Public Schools debate.

"At our last meeting we assigned topics for our winter quarter series, Issues in America." Bob Eubanks, the Adult Elective Class team leader, was getting the planning session started. "Marie and John, since you're responsible for the first session in the unit, why don't you remind us of your subject and share your tentative lesson plan."

"Our topic is Church, State, and Public Schools," Marie began," an issue which hasn't hit our community yet. Nor, I suspect, if we 'ran it up the flagpole,' would anybody salute. So I've prepared this ten-item opinionnaire to begin the session to see if I can motivate the group right away *(method A3b)*. Here's a copy of my creation for everyone." The team members filled out the opinionnaire hurriedly and looked it over.

"Are you going to tell me how many I got right?" Sam Wilson asked jokingly.

"Afraid not, Sam. You'll find out in class Sunday."

OPINIONNAIRE REPORT FORM

	1	2	3	4	5	6	7	8	9	10
YES										
NO										

METHODS USED

Opinionnaire (A3b)

WHAT'S YOUR OPINION?
CHURCH, STATE, AND PUBLIC SCHOOLS

State your opinion by writing "yes" or "no" in the blanks *before and after* each numbered statement. Tear off the numbered section on the left side and turn it in to be counted.

_____ 1. Teachers should lead students in the praying of the Lord's Prayer to open each school day. ____

_____ 2. School district psychologists should serve parochial school students when their services are needed. ____

_____ 3. Students should be transported from public schools to churches for religious instruction in public school buses. ____

_____ 4. Choral directors may explain the religious meaning of music sung in an objective fashion. ____

_____ 5. Students who do not want to participate in an opening exercise which includes the reading of the Bible should be able to excuse themselves. ____

_____ 6. A public school district should provide math textbooks for parochial schools in its area. ____

_____ 7. Students should be excused from saluting the American flag in a school ceremony if doing so is against their religious or moral convictions. ____

_____ 8. Religion is a subject which may be a part of a public high school's curriculum. ____

_____ 9. Parochial school students should be able to take some of their classes at public school rather than "all or none." ____

_____ 10. History teachers must not explain doctrines of religious groups even though they were major influences in historical events. ____

Lesson Planning
Example Three

Marie turned her attention back to the group. "What do you think of this as an opener?" Everyone nodded in agreement. "Good. However, my loyal husband disagrees. He thinks that there is more interest than knowledge and wants to focus attention on the heart of the problem with a skit." All eyes turned to John, who handed out his skit *(method A2b).*

"Marie, being an attorney, zeroed in on more issues than I knew about, and I've been in school work for more years than I'll admit," John began. "She's done her homework. I've just pointed up the most troublesome issue, pluralism."

Sam spoke for the group: "John, I didn't know you had such a creative sense of humor. Don't ask us to choose—let's use both of these openers!" The smiles and nods supported Sam's opinion.

"O.K., then, let's let them work on the opinionnaire as they arrive, rip off the turn-in portions, and then we'll have the skit and reaction." John turned to Marie as he finished his sentence.

(continued on p. 75)

Fold up until character is introduced.

Skit Analysis (A2b)

A MEETING TO REMEMBER

Chair: I, the chair, call this school board meeting to order. Each of you represents a certain number of voters. Introduce yourselves and your number of voters. When you vote *that's* the number you'll have.

Stant: I'm P. Roto Stant—541 voters.

Theist: I'm A. E. Theist—7 voters.

O'Lick: I'm Cathy O'Lick—121 voters.

Brew: I'm H. E. Brew—111 voters.

Hammed: I'm Mo Hammed—398 voters.

Chair: The issue is whether or not to have a religious as well as a patriotic ceremony to open each school day.

Theist: I vote against the religious exercise. My voters object to such indoctrination.

Brew: We find that totally unacceptable, A. E. I move that we have scripture reading from what my Christian friends call the "Old Testament," because both our constituencies consider it sacred.

O'Lick: *(Agreeing)* I'm with you, Brew. I also move that we use the shorter version of the Lord's Prayer, because it's biblical and could be considered Jewish, too.

Stant: Look friends *(standing up),* it'll be the New Testament and the long Lord's Prayer, because I've got the votes! So there!!

Theist: That's not fair!

Rubble: *(Entering)* Sorry I'm late but I've listened to the meeting over the radio. I'm T. Rubble—244 voters. I agree wholeheartedly with Stant about the Bible and prayers. And since my 244 voters, who moved into the new apartment complex last month, are of the same general persuasion as Hammed over there, who has 398 votes, we've agreed to cast our 642 votes for daily readings from the Koran. Now we can discuss what prayer to use. I, too, believe in majority rule!

Lesson Planning Example Three

Marie said, "At this point we believe that I should give a lecture on what the court decisions have been up to this point. This is my lecture outline" *(method B1a)*.

The team studied the outline and Deb Jacks said, "It seems to cover all the points brought out in the opinionnaire. I assume that after your lecture you'll answer class members' questions."

(continued on p. 76)

IN CASE OF
ATOMIC ATTACK,
DO NOT PRAY
UNTIL YOU
LEAVE SCHOOL.
IT'S ILLEGAL HERE!

Lecture (B1a)

CHURCH, STATE AND PUBLIC SCHOOLS

Introduction: Cartoon showing poster at public school—"In case of atomic attack, do not pray until you leave school. It's illegal here!" Why?

I. Why the first amendment was written (1791)
   A. European precedent
   B. The Colonial situation
II. The degree to which the amendment was obeyed in the schools
   A. The Protestant bias of the early public schools
   B. Roman Catholic challenge: N. Y. state
   C. The parochial school response to "godless" (religiously neutral) schools
III. The significant cases
   A. Pierce vs. Sisters, 1924, the right to parochial education
   B. McCullum vs. Illinois, 1948, sectarian religion not to be taught in the schools
   C. Various cases, the rights of schools to cooperate in released-time religious education off school property
   D. Schempp vs. Abington Twp., 1963, the illegality of the praying of the Lord's Prayer. The attempt of the NY State Regents to prepare a nonsectarian prayer: "Almighty God, we acknowledge our dependence upon Thee and we beg Thy blessings upon us, our parents, our teachers, and our country." Conclusion: any prayer is sectarian.
   E. The "child-benefit" theory of the Supreme Court and its applications
   F. Acceptable "religious" activities

Conclusion: "Shared time" expresses the court's views, i.e., *both* the parents and states have rights.

Marie agreed. "John will tabulate the opinionnaires while I talk, and I can present the results of the opinionnaire and then answer the inevitable questions for as long as time permits. I'll have a few questions prepared in case they're needed" (*method B2b*).

Chairman Eubanks quipped, "Assuming you survive all the emotion you arouse, how do you plan to conclude this session?"

Marie replied, "On this John and I also agree: we'd like to break the class into three groups by the school districts represented. Each group will assess the degree to which its schools are following the law, and, if there are serious infractions, they will prepare a position statement to consider presenting to the school board *(method C1b)*. Of course, minority opinions will be included."

"We believe," John continued, "that the statements should be presented next week." (They were.)

Question and Answer (B2b)

1. What would be the psychological effects on your children if they heard another religion's scriptures read and its prayers prayed daily?

2. What activities in the home or school could make up for the benefits of Bible reading and prayer moved out of the public school? What are the benefits?

3. If you were a federal judge, how would you explain "pluralism" to a 12-year-old? Or, how would you explain its effects on Bible use in the school to your child?

LESSON PLANNING EXAMPLE 3

The Lesson Plan Used by Marie and John for *Church, State, and Public Schools*

Objectives: 1. The students will be able to define or illustrate "pluralism."

                 2. The students will be able to (a) identify and (b) take a position on two current issues in the Church, State, and Public Schools debate.

CLOCK TIME	METHODS	IN CHARGE	MATERIALS NEEDED
9:40	Give out and start pupils on opinionnaires.	Marie	Duplicated copies of the opinionnaire and pencils
9:50	Welcome, take up the opinionnaire tear-offs, and pray opening prayer.	Marie	
9:55	Skit	John and classmates	Copies of the skit given ahead of time, prepared name tags to hang around neck
10:00	Lecture (John tallies opinionnaire results and copies on newsprint.)	Marie	Newsprint and marker
10:20	Opinionnaire report posted	John	
10:22	Answer questions.	Marie	
10:30	Form groups by school districts represented. Work on position statements until time for worship.	John	
10:30	Mizpah benediction (Those who wish to work on are encouraged to do so.)		

A2b

Skit Analysis

A3b

Opinionnaire

begin with MOTIVATION and DISCOVERY

B1a

Lecture

develop by PRESENTATION and ELABORATION

B2b

Question & Answer

C1b

Position Statement

conclude with APPLICATION

POSTSCRIPT

A Message to: (1) Beginning teachers/leaders who have studied **TEACH**NIQUES
(2) Persons who have taught **TEACH**NIQUES in classes for new teacher/leaders

From: The Author

I would like to have your reactions to **TEACH**NIQUES to help me in my work as a professor, pastor, and writer of books for teachers of various levels. I need to know what you've found helpful and not helpful in this book, especially the **TEACH**NIQUE approach of the methods pages with DEFINITIONS, DESIGN, DIRECTIONS on one side and EXAMPLES and EXERCISES on the other.

Thus, I have prepared a questionnaire on page 79 for beginning teachers/leaders and another questionnaire on page 80 for trainers of beginning teachers. I would be most grateful if you would fill out as much of the appropriate questionnaire as you wish to and mail it to me with any additional comments you'd like to add. Send it to:

Dr. Jack Renard Presseau
c/o John Knox Press
341 Ponce de Leon, N.E.
Atlanta, GA 30365
U. S. A.

One of the most helpful experiences of my life was the flurry of letters I received from those who read and studied in elective classes my book, *I'm Saved, You're Saved— Maybe,* also published by John Knox Press. In being an interim pastor (which I am, typically) or in leading teacher training workshops for churches and regional training events, I have found grassroots feedback most instructive whether the comments were complimentary or negatively critical. Those who have shared their insights with me have helped me better to perform my vocation as a Christian educator, a teacher. For your questionnaire with its insights I thank you in advance.

TEACHNIQUES: Questionnaire for Teachers/Leaders of Youth and Adults

Please print or type.

Name _____

Street or
Route & Box # _____

State _____ ZIP_____

Country _____

Denomination _____

HOW DID YOU GET **TEACH**NIQUES?
____ I purchased it. ____ Church got it.

____ Other (explain) _____

_____

IN WHAT PROGRAM DO YOU TEACH?
                        (Approximate Age Range)
Church School Youth   ____ 12–15 ____ 16–18
Youth "Fellowship"   ____ 12–15 ____ 16–18

Other Youth (explain) _____

_____

Adults ____ male ____ female ____ both
(Ages) ____ 18–30 ____ 30–45 ____45–65 ____65+
____ Men's Group   ____ Adult Church School
____ Women's Group____ Adult Informal Group

____ Other_____

WITH WHOM WILL YOU TEACH?
____ Part of a team
____ By myself
____ One experienced "lead" teacher

____ Other (explain) _____

_____

HOW ARE YOU (WILL YOU BE) TRAINED TO TEACH?
____ No training
____ In a course given by my church of
    ____ 1 ____ 2 ____ 3 ____ 4 ____5+ sessions
____ Course given by my denomination in my area
____ Course taken at a summer conference

____ Other (explain) _____

_____

CHURCH SCHOOL TEACHERS, WHAT CURRICULUM DO YOU USE?
____ The "International" or "Uniform" lessons
____ My denomination's, but not "Uniform"

____ Other (name it) _____

_____

CHECK ITEMS YOUR TEACHING ROOM HAS:
____ Movable chairs ____ Bibles
____ Movable tables ____ Bible dictionary
____ Bulletin board ____ Concordance
____ Chalkboard   ____ Commentary
____ Bible land maps____ Theological wordbook

CHECK THOSE ITEMS WHICH YOU HAVE:
____ Commentary ____ Bible dictionary
____ Concordance ____ Theological wordbook
____ Curriculum materials
____ Commentary on the Uniform Lessons

____ Other (name) _____

EVALUATE HELPFULNESS OF **TEACH**NIQUES:

	Great	Good	Fair	Poor
Flow-chart approach	____	____	____	____
Method directions	____	____	____	____
Method examples	____	____	____	____
Method exercises	____	____	____	____
Understandability	____	____	____	____

WHAT DID YOU LIKE THE MOST?

WHAT DID YOU LIKE THE LEAST?

CHECK WHAT YOU'D LIKE IN A FUTURE BOOK FOR TEACHERS:
____ More methods for the nine categories
____ More methods categories
____ Bible study methods
____ Help with using Bible reference books
____ Help with involving students
____ Help with specific problems, such as . . .

_____

____ Other_____

_____

YOUR NOTE TO THE AUTHOR:

Thank you!

TEACHNIQUES: Questionnaire for Those Who Train Teachers of Youth and Adults

Please print or type.

Name _____

Street or
Route & Box # _____

State _____ ZIP _____

Country _____

Denomination _____

HOW DID YOU GET **TEACH**NIQUES?
____ I purchased it. ____ Church got it.

____ Other (explain) _____

_____

WHO ARE YOU? (Check all which apply.)
____ An experienced teacher
____ Department chairperson or superintendent
____ Part-time nonordained church educator
____ Full-time nonordained church educator
____ Minister
____ College professor
____ Seminary professor

____ Other (explain) _____

_____

WHO ARE YOUR PUPILS?
____ Lay teachers of youth church school
____ Lay teachers of adult church school
____ Youth fellowship leaders
____ College students
____ Seminary students
____ Church professionals

____ Other (explain) _____

_____

DESCRIBE THE TYPICAL SITUATION IN WHICH YOU USE **TEACH**NIQUES:

EVALUATE HELPFULNESS OF **TEACH**NIQUES:

	Great	Good	Fair	Poor
Flow-chart approach	____	____	____	____
Method directions	____	____	____	____
Method examples	____	____	____	____
Method exercises	____	____	____	____
Readability	____	____	____	____
Method categories	____	____	____	____
Sample lessons	____	____	____	____
Choice of methods	____	____	____	____

WHAT DID YOU LIKE THE MOST?

WHAT DID YOU LIKE THE LEAST?

CHECK WHAT YOU'D LIKE IN A FUTURE BOOK FOR TEACHERS:
____ More methods for the nine categories
____ More methods categories
____ Bible study methods
____ Help with using Bible reference books
____ Help with involving students
____ Methods of class self-evaluation
____ Teacher training models/lesson plans
____ Help with specific problems, such as . . .

_____

____ Other (explain) _____

_____

YOUR NOTE TO THE AUTHOR:

Thank you!